1991

White Noise, the story of a professor of Hitler studies and his family, was DeLillo's breakthrough book and has received much attention and critical acclaim. In the introduction to this volume, Frank Lentricchia provides an overview of the novel's critical reception, while examining it in the context of other works by Don DeLillo. The other essays in the volume discuss DeLillo's view of family and divorce, Hitler's role in the twentieth century, technology as a mortal threat, and postmodern America. This collection offers suggestive means by which to approach DeLillo's important contemporary work.

NEW ESSAYS ON WHITE NOISE

★ The American Novel ★

GENERAL EDITOR
Emory Elliott
University of California, Riverside

New Essays on
White Noise

Edited by

Frank Lentricchia

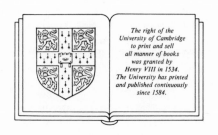

The right of the
University of Cambridge
to print and sell
all manner of books
was granted by
Henry VIII in 1534.
The University has printed
and published continuously
since 1584.

CAMBRIDGE UNIVERSITY PRESS

Cambridge

New York   Port Chester   Melbourne   Sydney

Published by the Press Syndicate of the University of Cambridge
The Pitt Building, Trumpington Street, Cambridge CB2 1RP
40 West 20th Street, New York, NY 10011, USA
10 Stamford Road, Oakleigh, Melbourne 3166, Australia

First published 1991

Printed in the United States of America

Library of Congress Cataloging-in-Publication Data
New essays on White noise / edited by Frank Lentricchia.
p. cm.
ISBN 0-521-39291-8 (hardcover).–ISBN 0-521-39893-2 (pbk.)
1. DeLillo, Don. White noise.   I. Lentricchia, Frank.
PS3554.E4425W4836   1991
813'PR.54–dc20   91-9267

British Library Cataloguing in Publication Data
New Essays on White noise.
I. Lentricchia, Frank   II. DeLillo, Don, *1936–*
813.54

ISBN 0–521–39291–8 hardback
ISBN 0–521–39893–2 paperback

To our students

Contents

Contents

5

Tales of the Electronic Tribe

Series Editor's Preface

In literary criticism the last twenty-five years have been particularly fruitful. Since the rise of the New Criticism in the 1950s, which focused attention of critics and readers upon the text itself – apart from history, biography, and society – there has emerged a wide variety of critical methods which have brought to literary works a rich diversity of perspectives: social, historical, political, psychological, economic, ideological, and philosophical. While attention to the text itself, as taught by the New Critics, remains at the core of contemporary interpretation, the widely shared assumption that works of art generate many different kinds of interpretation has opened up possibilities for new readings and new meanings.

Before this critical revolution, many American novels had come to be taken for granted by earlier generations of readers as having an established set of recognized interpretations. There was a sense among many students that the canon was established and that the larger thematic and interpretative issues had been decided. The task of the new reader was to examine the ways in which elements such as structure, style, and imagery contributed to each novel's acknowledged purpose. But recent criticism has brought these old assumptions into question and has thereby generated a wide variety of original, and often quite surprising, interpretations of the classics, as well as of rediscovered novels such as Kate Chopin's *The Awakening*, which has only recently entered the canon of works that scholars and critics study and that teachers assign their students.

The aim of The American Novel Series is to provide students of American literature and culture with introductory critical guides to

American novels now widely read and studied. Each volume is devoted to a single novel and begins with an introduction by the volume editor, a distinguished authority on the text. The introduction presents details of the novel's composition, publication history, and contemporary reception, as well as a survey of the major critical trends and readings from first publication to the present. This overview is followed by four or five original essays, specifically commissioned from senior scholars of established reputation and from outstanding younger critics. Each essay presents a distinct point of view, and together they constitute a forum of interpretative methods and of the best contemporary ideas on each text.

It is our hope that these volumes will convey the vitality of current critical work in American literature, generate new insights and excitement for students of the American novel, and inspire new respect for and new perspectives upon these major literary texts.

Emory Elliott
University of California, Riverside

1

Introduction

FRANK LENTRICCHIA

FOR OBVIOUS reasons Don DeLillo's publishers are pleased to advertise their man as a "highly acclaimed" novelist, but until the publication of *White Noise* in 1985 DeLillo was a pretty obscure object of acclaim, both in and out of the academy. His readings are rare. He attends no conferences, teaches no summer workshops in fiction writing, never shows up on late-night television and doesn't cultivate second-person narrative in the present tense. So he has done little to promote himself in the approved ways. And the books are hard: All of them expressions of someone who has ideas (I don't mean opinions), who reads things other than novels and newspapers (though he clearly reads those, too, and to advantage), and who experiments with literary convention.

What is characteristic about DeLillo's books, aside from their contemporary subjects, is their irredeemably heterogeneous texture; they are montages of tones, styles, and voices that have the effect of yoking together terror and wild humor as the essential tone of contemporary America. Terrific comedy is DeLillo's mode: even, at the most unexpected moments, in *Libra*, his imagination of the life of President John F. Kennedy's assassin, Lee Harvey Oswald. It is the sort of mode that marks writers who conceive their vocation as an act of cultural criticism; who invent in order to intervene; whose work is a kind of anatomy, an effort to represent their culture in its totality; and who desire to move readers to the view that the shape and fate of their culture dictates the shape and fate of the self.

In other words, writers like DeLillo are not the sort who are impressed by the representative directive of the literary vocation of our time, the counsel to "write what you know," taken to heart by

1

producers of the new regionalism who in the South, for example, claim parentage in Faulkner and Flannery O'Connor, two writers who would have been floored to hear that "what you know" means the chastely bound snapshot of your neighborhood and your biography. (An embarrassing sign of the aesthetic times: One critic, writing for the *Partisan Review,* reported his happy astonishment that DeLillo could invent such believable kids in *White Noise,* because, after all, DeLillo has no kids.) Writers in DeLillo's tradition have too much ambition to stay home. To leave home (I don't mean "transcend" it), to leave your region, your ethnicity, the idiom you grew up with, is made to seem pretentious in the setting of the new regionalism, and the South is not unique: It makes no difference if the province is generic North Carolina or generic New York City, or if the provincialist is Reynolds Price or Jay McInerney. In the cultural setting in which Bobbie Ann Mason incarnates the idea of the writer and Frederick Barthelme succeeds his brother in the pages of the *New Yorker,* to write novels that might be titled *An American Tragedy* or *USA* – DeLillo's first book was called *Americana* (1971) – no doubt is pretentious. In this kind of setting, a writer who tries what DeLillo tries is simply immodest, shamelessly so. Apparently only the Latin Americans have earned the right to their immodesty. So American novelists and critics first look sentimentally to the other Americas, where (so it goes) the good luck of fearsome situations of social crisis encourages a major literature; then look ruefully to home, where (so it goes) the comforts of our stability require a minor, apolitical, domestic fiction of the triumphs and agonies of autonomous private individuals operating in "the private sector" of Raymond Carver and Anne Tyler, the modesty of small, good things: fiction all but labeled "No expense of intellect required. To be applied in eternal crises of the heart only." Unlike these new regionalists of and for the Reagan eighties, DeLillo (or Joan Didion, or Toni Morrison, or Cynthia Ozick, or Norman Mailer) offers us no myth of political virginity preserved, no "individuals" who are not expressions of – and responses to – specific historical processes.

But things are changing now for DeLillo: In 1984 he was given an award by the American Academy and Institute of Arts and

Letters that honored his work to date; then *White Noise* won the American Book Award for 1985; then *Libra* was made a main selection of the Book-of-the-Month Club in the spring of 1988, hit the best-seller list for several weeks in the summer of that year, and got its author invited to do interviews on National Public Radio and NBC's *Today* show. Uncharacteristically, *Libra*'s author assented. And best sign of all of cultural relevance in our day: The media political right has begun to take an active interest in DeLillo. The "highly acclaimed" author is now, in his newfound visibility, drawing his harshest notices.

In the midst of a presidential campaign in which he usually devoted his nationally syndicated column to the vagaries of George Bush and Michael Dukakis, George Will took time out to write an article on *Libra* in which he called DeLillo a literary vandal for writing about real people, a bad citizen for suggesting that Kennedy's murder was not the act of a "lone gunman" but the production of a conspiracy, and a bad influence because a lot of people were now apparently reading DeLillo. Will's charge of literary vandalism and bad citizenship (What is this, anyway, China?) is the latest frightened judgment – with a long American history – delivered upon writers critically engaged with particular American cultural and political matters, writers with terminal bad manners who refuse to limit themselves to celebratory platitudes about the truths of the heart, and who don't respect the definitive shibboleth of literary culture since the eighteenth century – the sharp and deadly distinction between fiction and nonfiction: as if everyone didn't know who Dreiser was writing about when *An American Tragedy* came out; as if Dos Passos hadn't named and butchered some famous names in *USA*; as if Doctorow's *Ragtime*, Coover's *Public Burning*, and Mailer's *Executioner's Song* hadn't worked that same territory.

Will is no lone gunman either: A few weeks before, a Pulitzer prize–winning columnist for the *Washington Post*, who writes under the name of Jonathan Yardley, had similarly described DeLillo's efforts to imagine the lives of real people as "beneath contempt." Yardley is angry because he thinks DeLillo has somehow cheated, that thanks to a conspiracy of literary radicals he has "quite inexplicably acquired a substantial literary reputation"; Yardley is convinced that *Libra* "will be lavishly praised in those quarters where DeLillo's ostentatiously gloomy view of American life and culture is embraced"; and he is worried because Oswald, like James Dean and Marilyn Monroe, continues to fascinate us, Yardley included. Brandishing the literary theory of Eudora Welty, Cumaean sibyl of the new regionalism, who declares that fiction must have a "private address," Yardley accuses DeLillo of committing an "ideological fiction." By ideology he means (on this he's as "liberal" as he is "conservative") any point of view which traces any problematic action to an institutional, structural, or collective cause, rather than a personal one: any theory of society which refuses the lone gunman explanation of anything, but particularly of social crisis. Or, as Will puts it: DeLillo's is "yet another exercise in blaming America for Oswald's act of derangement." But political fiction is not fiction that forsakes the personal in order to blame the public sector, which it surely does critically assess; it is fiction that refuses the opposition of the personal and public altogether. Since DeLillo does not produce happy evaluations of the effects of large public pressures on individuals – has any interesting writer in America ever done so? – it follows for the media political right, which believes that America is good and that only individuals go astray (the homeless bring it on themselves, as Reagan used to say), that DeLillo is something of a traitor to his country.

In the words of a *New Criterion* soldier who preceded both Will and Yardley in this vein, DeLillo thinks "contemporary American society is the worst enemy that the cause of human individuality and self-realization has ever had." The reality is otherwise, at least as it is seen in the *New Criterion*. Here in America we lead "richly varied" lives: If we do not, if there is any fault to be found, if anyone "is guilty of turning modern Americans into xerox copies, it is Don DeLillo." Two cheers for the media right: Their censorious reflections on DeLillo's work – what consequences, anyway, ought to be visited upon the writer whose acts of invention are termed bad citizenship and bad influence? – are the best backhanded testimony I've seen in a long time on behalf of the social power of literature, for good or for ill, and an unintended but superb compliment to DeLillo's success in making his writing count beyond the elite circle of connoisseurs of postmodernist criticism and fiction. Not wanting to say so, the media right has nevertheless said in so many words, against its Will, that fiction does not have a private address and that DeLillo does to Oswald what we, for good or for ill, do every day to our friends, lovers, and enemies: He interprets him, he creates a character.

The telling assumption of DeLillo's media-right reviewers is that he is coming from the left – as if the criticism of American culture is necessarily a Marxist plot and we've never heard of the activists on the political right and their agendas for social change; as if some of our most honored writers – I mean precisely those whom conservative intellectuals charge universities with forsaking, as we go whoring after the strange gods of minority cultures – as if Emerson, Thoreau, and Twain had not written savage critiques of America, not peripherally but centrally, as their life's work. It is true that DeLillo's heroes are usually in repulsed flight from American life. But what did Emerson say? He said: "Society" – he meant ours – "is a joint stock company in conspiracy against the manhood of every one of its members."

Should conservative intellectuals refresh their memories of American literature, they'd find that the canonical American writers – those who conservatives say best embody American values – are adversarial critics of our culture. The American literary way has from the start been fiercely antinomian, suspicious, even "paranoid," and how interesting that key word of contemporary jargon becomes when it characterizes the main take on our culture from Anne Hutchinson and Emerson to Pynchon and DeLillo. The main literary line is political, but not in the trivial didactic sense of offering programs of renovation, or of encouraging us to go out and "do something." Writing in the main line in effect stands in harsh judgment against American fiction of the last couple of decades, that soft humanist underbelly of American literature: a realism of domestic setting whose characters play out their little dramas of ordinary event and feeling in an America miraculously free from the environment and disasters of contemporary technology, untouched by racial and gender tensions, and blissfully unaware of political power; a fiction, to be sure, cleverly veneered with place (Tyler's Baltimore), brand names, and other signs of advanced consumer culture (Carver's cube steak, his Jim Beam). In the fashioning of such surfaces lies the entire claim of these writers to realism. But the deep action of this kind of fiction is culturally and historically rootless, an expression of the possibilities of "human nature," here, now, forever, as ever. This is realism maybe in the old philosophical sense of the word, when they affirmed that only the universals are real. The Jim Beam, the dope, the TV set, the cube steak, which all make apparently authoritative appearances in Carver's world, are not of the essence; they are merely props. In the context of recent American fiction, the reading of DeLillo's writing is an experience of overwhelming cultural density – these are novels that could not have been written before the mid-1960s. In this, their historical rigor, I suspect, lies their political outrage: the unprecedented degree to which they prevent their readers from gliding off into the comfortable sentiment that the real problems of the human race have always been about what they are today.

In the lingo of the publishing trade, *White Noise* was DeLillo's "breakthrough" book, a term I first heard applied to the novel by a salesman from Viking who made the claim shortly after the book was published. (In other words, when it was too early to make the claim.) He was saying that the novel would achieve more than the critical esteem which would "butter no parsnips," as Robert Frost once put it, and he turned out to be right. The novel sold much better than DeLillo's previous seven and in a short time found acceptance in the very place held up to satiric scrutiny in *White Noise*, the place in America where serious fiction is read, discussed, and written about. With *White Noise*, DeLillo has cracked the university curriculum in American literature, more and more taking over the slot hitherto occupied by a novelist beloved by students and professors in the sixties and seventies, Thomas Pynchon. The book orders of university teachers do what critical esteem cannot do: butter the parsnips while making, sustaining, and unmaking reputations – even of the canonical sort.

The question as to why a particular novel "breaks through" to a mass audience is subject to very little evidence of the hard kind and therefore to much speculation, as in the following: (1) Ours is a country committed to mass education, even at the higher levels, and *White Noise* is a campus novel (of sorts). (2) DeLillo has pretty assiduously stayed away from the domestic novel and the complacent realism regularly featured in the *New Yorker* and the *Atlantic*, fiction "around-the-house-and-in-the-backyard," as he once put it. In an age of domestic realism, writers who do not comply must expect to pay the price. But in *White Noise*, DeLillo finally writes his domestic novel (of sorts). (3) *White Noise* is DeLillo's eighth novel. To that point he was well known to reviewers and a cadre of readers as a gifted writer who had published seven novels in the space of a decade. By the time of *White Noise*, DeLillo's career has gathered some momentum, is poised at the edge of breakthrough, if only he will write the right sort of novel. (4) The central event of *White Noise* is an ecological disaster. Thus: an ecological novel at the dawn of ecological consciousness. (5) The inevitable anecdotal reports, two of which I can't resist passing on: In a course on contemporary fiction, one of my colleagues tells me that a student said to him, "This is the first book in the course about me." Another undergraduate tells me that he did not "read" *White Noise*; he "inhaled" it.

The speculation I favor is the one about the domestic novel, a sentimental form plied to huge profit by women novelists in America in the nineteenth century (Updike, Carver, and company have learned the mode well), Anne Tyler's work being only its latest commercial avatar. In *White Noise*, DeLillo deploys that popular literary form of the private life, but only in order to have his way with it, showing what large and nearly invisible things invade our kitchens, the various coercive environments within which the so-called private life is led. And yet though he insists in *White Noise*, as everywhere else in his work, upon a comprehensive cultural canvas, and though his critical impulses here, as everywhere else in his work, give no quarter, there remains in his fiction a space for the poetry of mystery, awe, and commitment; in *White Noise*, a commitment to the possibility, however laid to waste by contemporary forces, of domesticity as the life support we cannot do without. The formal handles that *White Noise* gives its readers are easy to grab on to; its texture is inviting, often hilariously so. But this novel, like all of his books, is an original, and like all originals resists being taken in by conventional categories; is therefore hard to talk about with justice done to the thing itself; remains necessarily, and delightfully, elusive, but not beyond reach.

Whatever the reasons for its commercial success, *White Noise* represents no radical departure from its author's uncommercial earlier work. From the beginning DeLillo has been interested in bending traditional forms to his will and to the life of his culture. *Americana* (1971), his first novel, is a road book, picaresque in trajectory, the man on the road an exile from New York's media world, with a movie camera in tow – a cool, ironic first-person narrator, like Jack Gladney in *White Noise*, who is nevertheless (again like Gladney) not really in control. *End Zone* (1972) plays off the genre of the sports novel, its first-person narrator a startling combination of football star and searching intellectual, taking courses in the theories and strategies of nuclear war, and who, like all of DeLillo's narrators and many of his major characters, moves, with seeming inevitability, from satire to primitive terror, from detached acerbic observation to rapturous lyric commitment, from the full glare of public space to the intense isolation and ascetic discipline of private space: a stripped-down small room, a man in the process of withdrawal, brooding, losing his mind. In the last pages of the novel the narrator/halfback of *End Zone* is carried off to the infirmary in a catatonic state, to be fed intravenously. *Great Jones Street* (1973), a kind of sequel to *End Zone*, begins with another figure in the eye of publicity, a rock singer of megastar proportions, who suddenly and mysteriously drops off the tour in order to hole up in a badly run-down room in Greenwich Village, a hermitage soon violated by various figures on the make, representing businesses legitimate and otherwise, seeking to return the product to market and to turn even his acts of resistance, especially his acts of resistance, into a commodity.

After the rush of three books in three years (the first a while in the making), there is a three-year gap, and then DeLillo's most formally adventurous work (it wouldn't do to call it a novel) appears in 1976. *Ratner's Star*, a takeoff on science fiction, in its first two-thirds is Menippean satire via Lewis Carroll's Alice books, a meditation on the modern scientific mind, its hunger for abstraction becoming under DeLillo's gaze a direct route to madness and the self-reveling grotesqueness which demands the cartoon representation that he gives it. In its last third – an abrupt shift in generic gears – *Ratner's Star* is a recollection of Joyce's narrative methods in *Ulysses*, an exploration of the undergrounds of several consciousnesses, managed with the montage-like cuts of the filmmaker and sudden, deliberately unprepared shifts from third-person narration to first. The frequent descents into psychological interiors culminate in the last, apocalyptic pages of the book in an actual descent – an all-out race on a bicycle by the Nobel prize–winning teenage central character for an actual hole in the ground, the end of his terror-ridden race the catatonia that in DeLillo's fiction appears culturally necessary. In *Ratner's Star* he asks: "Are catatonic people setting a standard for the rest of us?" And a few pages later one of his characters responds as if announcing the prime rule of contemporary existence: "The only way to survive is to curtail one's perspective, to exist as close to one's center as possible."

In the two novels that follow *Ratner's Star* – *Players* (1977) and *Running Dog* (1978) – DeLillo turns his formal attention to the thriller mode and the manipulations thereof. In keeping with the character of the genre, these are swift, pared-down narratives that deploy topics of urgent contemporary political interest: terrorism and Wall Street in *Players;* government intelligence agencies, the Mafia, pornography dealers, hip journalists, and a U.S. senator in *Running Dog,* plotters all, all in search of an alleged orgiastic film made in the *Führerbunker* in Hitler's last days, starring the man himself. Both books are easy to read, but neither has earned much of a readership, probably because DeLillo insists on cutting the ground from under thriller-novel expectations. Gripping plots do not eventuate in final revelations but in endings of no romance, with romance-seeking major characters sunk in boredom or private quests, all goals frustrated, subplots not tied up – endings as nonendings, putting readers exactly in the place of his frustrated characters, asking them to reconsider their experience, return to the beginning, with all excitement deliberately drained off by the writer, and to read again, this time for reasons other than thrills. Such reconsideration will reveal DeLillo at his most playful, particularly in *Running Dog*, producing in the margins of that book a form of literary capriccio, variations on the role of film in contemporary consciousness: as commodity, as form of entertainment, as medium of Eros, and as the form of self-representation that defines postmodernism. Film: the chief artistic innovation of the twentieth century as both mode of representing experience and as experience itself, all the experience we can know – film *in* and film *as* consciousness.

Again, after three books in three years (*Ratner's Star* a while in the making), there is – given his work habits – a considerable gap, this one of four years, a period during which DeLillo lived in Greece and wrote his politically most ambitious novel, *The Names* (1982), a book set in Greece and various Middle East locales. *The Names* is shaped by a form virtually invented and perfected by Henry James – the international novel – and tried occasionally and bravely by American writers since (Hemingway in *The Sun Also Rises*, Fitzgerald in *Tender Is the Night*). Almost never achieved in the form is the textural richness that marks James's major books, in which the American innocent is set down in the alien context of Europe. James Axton, first-person narrator of *The Names*, undergoes what Henry James's American innocent cannot avoid: a tragic education beginning with the knowledge of his alien context and ending with knowledge of self, his own complicity, learning that what he thought and desired to be the horror of Old World otherness is more than matched by horrors belonging to American selfhood.

For sheer tonal thickness and range, DeLillo has not written before or since anything quite like *The Names*. Axton's narration is propelled as if by a voice of multiple personality: When in conversation with other Americans like himself, in the employ of the multinationals, he is all wit and sophistication; with his estranged wife, all irony and intimacy intertwined; with himself in meditation on landscape, the play of natural light, Athens, airports, Greek architecture, the holy places of Islam, the sights and especially the sounds of the Middle East – the sounds of the Arabic tongue – he gives us long and frequent stretches of prose poetry, a lyrical language so evocative that it overcomes the headlong push of narrative time with sensuous, ecstatic, plot-stopping reverie. Literally plot-stopping: displacing story, as if Axton needed to repress the plot that will eventually catch him up in his search for the meaning and the perpetrators of a series of cult murders. Axton's lyric poetry is an effort to escape from what fascinates as it closes in on him; a desire for the innocence that neither his work nor his culture will permit him – lyricism as a literate, connoisseur's form of catatonia – and his final understanding of the murderers is of a madness driven by similar lyric need: to stop history, to get out of a world made dense, diverse, and too present by polyglot pressures and modern technology; to hammer human being back into the soil; to become rooted again in order to live as close to our centers as possible.

Three years after *The Names*, DeLillo published *White Noise*, a culminating book: a first-person narrator, ironical and lyrical; the electronic media, particularly television; futuristic drugs; the power of consumer culture to revolt and seduce; popular culture in various guises; plots, novelistic and conspiratorial; the dauntingly precocious child, first seen in *Ratner's Star* and then in *The Names*; shadowy networks of power and control; the poetic lure of modern jargons from science, sports, and Madison Avenue – all of these elements feed into *White Noise* in order to form the insidious environment of DeLillo's contemporary family, Jack and Babette Gladney and their children from several marriages. And many of these elements, in different combinations, now fixated with a purity never before glimpsed in his writing – an obsession with obsession – are transmuted into the shape of his most popular and critically admired work to date: *Libra* (1988).

DeLillo's latest novel is a work reminiscent of the nonfiction novels of Truman Capote (*In Cold Blood*) and Norman Mailer (*The Executioner's Song*). *Libra* is also a recent variant of the novel of social fate, the so-called naturalist novel now rewritten inside the postmodern arena, in the society of the image: Lee Harvey Oswald and John Fitzgerald Kennedy, media born and baptized as triple-named assassin and victim. Like Emma in Flaubert's *Madame Bovary* and Carrie in Dreiser's *Sister Carrie*, Oswald and Kennedy are the playthings of the illusions that their cultures nurture and sustain, "character" wanting to be "image." But they are more: In DeLillo's imagination of them, they are the founding characters of postmodern America. DeLillo's Oswald gives strange new meaning to advice given to Jack Gladney in his desperate hour: "Kill to live."

White Noise garnered more reviews, by far, than any of DeLillo's previous books. Many of the reviewers – in a crucial act of self-fulling prophecy – made the point that *White Noise* was his most "accessible" novel, a relative judgment, of course, which many book-buyers, to Viking's delight, must have taken absolutely. And a number of reviewers – some of them the same who claimed the novel's accessibility – made the more-than-related point that *White Noise* is DeLillo's "warmest" novel. In an age of domestic realism, "warmth" is the definition of literary accessibility, family-oriented writing the direct route to lucidity. And the point about "warmth" is made not just by the sentimentalists among DeLillo's reviewers, in the act of welcoming him "home," into the mainstream, but – best testimony I know to the cultural power of domestic realism over the past couple of decades – by those who value DeLillo precisely for his against-the-grain style.

The reviewer who praises him for being that "rarest of birds, a novelist on fire with ideas," who says that in comparison to "DeLillo's large and terrifying talent, most modern fiction seems trifling indeed," this same reviewer will conclude by saying that *White Noise* is a "far greater book than *End Zone*, in large part because it is something more than cold and curious reason; it offsets its existential shivers with a domestic strength that is touching and true. In the midst of all the Pandoran currents and forces that pulse through the dark is a family that is vulnerable, warm bodies that turn to each other for shelter." In a similar vein, the reviewer for the self-preeningly radical *Village Voice*, after saying a number of penetrating things about DeLillo's work, telling us in so many words why it resists "warm" reception, concludes by praising him for finally coming through with "convincing treatment of his characters' inner lives." *White Noise*, he says in his last sentence, "strikes at both head and heart." The *Village Voice* joins hands with a magazine whose very name touches off – however unjustly – an image of legendary staidness, the *Library Journal*, guide for those who order books for libraries, and whose reviewer concludes that

White Noise is DeLillo's "warmest novel, and perhaps his best." And most revealingly: A longtime admirer, a weekday reviewer for the *New York Times*, characterizes DeLillo's sensibility as "icily intelligent," and then, caught up with his metaphor, proceeds to tell us why *White Noise* is so important: "It is almost as if we were listening to a massive glacier breaking up." Thus does DeLillo become "readable," thus does he reach his "peak."

Not everyone saw the novel so reductively, or so positively. Major reviewers in major places – the Sunday *New York Times*, the *New York Review of Books*, *Newsweek*, *Commonweal* – often made the point, with elegant concision, that DeLillo's focus is never "character" in isolation, but institutions, culture, the interdependence of the three, and the disturbing invasions of a self that would be autonomous. In *Commonweal*, Thomas DiPietro makes the most disturbing point of all, which if true – I think it is true – would seem surely to deny DeLillo consistent access to a large audience: "In DeLillo's truly Swiftean satire, we're never sure what he himself believes or what he thinks of his characters. As in Swift, we're instead forced to rely on ourselves, to measure literary experience against our own sense of reality."

But there is a complication in taking DeLillo in Swiftean terms, however seductive and telling the comparison. Swift did not tell his readers what he thought and believed because he could assume with confidence that those who could read him well shared his norms of reasonable behavior. DeLillo takes the Swiftean tack, but he cannot assume what Swift could assume, and there is the rub – the difficulty, for a democratic mass culture of diverse persuasions, of making sense out of what he writes. Like Ezra Pound before him, DeLillo needs a readership of the literarily endowed. Pound is extremely difficult, but no one should be shocked by the fact: After all, he wrote modernist poetry. But DeLillo writes the novel, the form which at the roots of its invention looked for a broad, middle-class reception and centrally, in order to gather that audience, has held up to it the mirror of "warm," bourgeois, family life.

The dissenters do not care for the Swiftean mode; they have no use for writers "on fire with ideas"; they do not buy the line that in *White Noise* DeLillo joins head and heart. The reviewer for *Time* complains, "Discovering malevolence in things and systems rather then in people is a little callow." It goes without saying that people are ultimately responsible for the "things and systems" they create. And it also goes without saying – one of the ironic themes of *White Noise* – that people have a hard time recognizing their faces in the mirror of modern technology, no doubt because they never wanted their technological revolutions to get out of control, assume a malevolent, undesirable life of their own, become virtually self-governing, like nature itself.

The aforementioned Yardley picks up the theme of the *Time* reviewer, what deserves to be called "happy humanism." Yardley thinks DeLillo is "prodigiously gifted," a "writer of stupendous talents" – superlatives quickly followed by phrases of bitter disappointment. *White Noise* is "another of DeLillo's exercises in fiction as political tract"; he's a "pamphleteer, not a novelist, he's interested in ideas and institutions . . . but not in people." His books are "dazzling" but "heartless" – "empty" at their "core": "Until he has something to say that comes from the heart rather than the evening news, his novels will fall far short of his talents." And so on. The best response to Yardley that I've seen came in Diane Johnson's *New York Review of Books* piece, where, taking him on directly, she reminds him that without "a willingness to engage the problems of the world around him we would not have the novels of Dickens, just as, without an acid tone and interest in abstraction, we would not have the novels of Voltaire." The difficulty with Yardley's complaint, she concludes, would seem to "lie in the definition of fiction." She deadpans it, she does not say "narrow" or "silly." Among reviewers of *White Noise*, Johnson deserves the last word with this intriguing sentence: "In all his work he seems less angry or disappointed than some critics of society, as if he had expected less in the first place, or perhaps his marvelous power with words is compensation for him." Impulses aesthetic and critical have – classically – stood in starkest opposition, but they go together in the modernist idea of literature, perhaps no more seamlessly than in Don DeLillo, last of the modernists, who takes for his critical object of aesthetic concern the postmodern situation.

2

Whole Families Shopping at Night!

THOMAS J. FERRARO

1

ONE of the first and most sustained teases in *White Noise*, Don DeLillo's stinging appreciation of the contemporary American family, concerns the genealogies of the children who reside with narrator Jack Gladney and his current wife, called simply Babette. "Babette and I and our children by previous marriages live at the end of a quiet street in what was once a wooded area with deep ravines," announces Jack on the second page. Which children by what previous marriages? A not unreasonable question, the reader assumes, especially given that the novel revolves around the daily life of the household, and that each of these children (even the still mostly silent toddler) is an important character in the book. For the reader whose curiosity has been provoked (and by DeLillo's design it has), it will take a novel-long information hunt to sort out the relations persisting among the Gladneys. In Chapter 2, a family lunch introduces the names of four children but not their descent lines. By Chapter 11, a careful reader has determined that there are indeed only four children – two boys, two girls – and that one of the boys and one of the girls are offspring of Jack, the other boy and girl are offspring of Babette. It takes considerably longer to determine who the other parent of each child in the house is, where these other parents live and what they do, and what offspring of Jack and Babette not in residence exist; and, by my tracking, we do not receive the last set of details (a schema of Jack's marital history) until Chapter 28, a full two-thirds through the novel.

The identification of Denise's father illustrates this mode of narrating family history:

> When I got home, Bob Pardee was in the kitchen practicing his golf swing. Bob is Denise's father. He said he was driving through town on his way to Glassboro to make a presentation and thought he'd take us all to dinner. (56)

Pardee's impromptu visit signifies not so much the amicability of Bob and Babette's divorce as the inconsequential nature of being an ex-husband and a father – and, ipso facto, the triviality of the information that one is an ex-husband or a father. Bob "pops in" on Jack; the report of the visit "drops into" the narrative, and the fact of Bob's paternity "flashes by" us. The matters of intercourse and procreation, of lineage and place, that for someone like Faulkner would be the founding, inexorable blood-knowledge of existence itself seem for Jack and the others to be pieces of trivia, the flotsam and jetsam of circumstance.[1]

DeLillo has configured the family trees of the children living in the Gladney house to parody the state of the domestic art in contemporary middle America: Heinrich, fourteen, from the marriage of Jack to Janet Savory (who as Mother Devi runs a profitable ashram in Tubb, Montana); Denise, eleven, from the marriage of Babette to Bob Pardee (who raises money for the legal defense fund of the nuclear industry); Steffie, a couple or so years younger than Denise, from the marriage of Jack and Dana Breedlove (who is a CIA courier in the third world); and Wilder, two, from the marriage of Babette to an unnamed "researcher" in the outback of Australia. Heinrich has a sister living with their mother; Wilder has a brother living with their father; Jack has at least one more daughter (Bee) from his middle wife (Tweedy Browner). We learn no details whatsoever of the circumstances of remarriage or the strategies behind the redistribution of children that went into the making of the Gladney household or its many satellites.

What emerges is a fearful symmetry. Each adult lives with a third or fourth spouse, a son from a previous marriage, a daughter from a different previous marriage, a stepson from one of the latest spouse's previous marriages, and a stepdaughter from another of that spouse's previous marriages. Every child lives with one progenitor, that parent's current mate, one half-sibling of the opposite

16

sex whose other parent lives elsewhere, and a combination of stepsister and stepbrother who are only half-siblings to one another. *Each* adult lives therefore with five other people whose average relation to him or her is only 20 percent; *every* child lives with five other people whose average relation to him or her is only 15 percent; and *everyone* in the household lives with five other people, *each of whom* is related on average by no more than (the same) 20 percent to *everyone else* in the house. Not a single child whom Babette has borne or whom Jack has fathered, whether in their custody or not, is living with both parents or even a full brother or sister. Above all, the current assemblage has not been together longer than Wilder's two years of age, and in all probability less than that.   *instability!*

Although we are not privileged to a single detail of "how Jack met Babette," it takes only Jack's own marital summary to give a sense of how serious these matters stand among them:

> My first and fourth marriages were to Dana Breedlove, who is Steffie's mother. The first marriage worked well enough to encourage us to try again as soon as it became mutually convenient. When we did, after the melancholy epochs of Janet Savory and Tweedy Browner, things proceeded to fall apart. But not before Stephanie Rose was conceived, a star-hung night in Barbados. Dana was there to bribe an official. (213)   *→ tone!*

marriage + procreation= casual

The narrative voice here is reminiscent of the dry naturalism that Pynchon uses for the "whole sick crew" sections of *V.*, and the figure of directionless movement that governs those sections — what Pynchon terms, "yo-yoing" — would serve for the rhythms of caprice ("mutual convenience") characterizing engagement, disengagement, and human issue among Jack, Dana, Janet, Tweedy, and (it seems) other members of the intelligence community working to destabilize unfriendly governments in underdeveloped countries.[2] To say that Jack has a tone resembling Pynchon's is to underscore here both his deprecatory self-irony ("the first marriage worked well enough") and, more importantly, the sarcastic way in which he deflates older forms of rhetoric ("a star-hung night in Barbados") to signify the deflation in the action itself (conceiving and by implication receiving a child so nonchalantly): I think Jack is aware that the impersonal constructions — "things

17

proceeded to fall apart" – beg the questions of concerted vision and responsibility, but, he is saying, in our world these simply are no longer questions.

The subjects of past spouses, scattered siblings, and the like come up every so often, but invariably as a form of parent–child interaction in which a parent or (in the funny and touching reversals of DeLillo's fabulous dialogue) child demonstrates sensitivity, as a small diversion with just enough tension to be entertaining (allowing for some fine one-liners), or as part of the game of "complete disclosure" through which Jack and Babette program their intimacy. All the Gladneys "interact" by any standard criteria extremely well with one another, cooperatively and in concert, with admirable degrees of both mutual insight and self-irony. Even Bee's Christmas stay, the visit by Babette's father, and the surprise appearances by Tweedy Browner and Bob Pardee generate only the mildest degree of anxiety, just enough to convince us that massive repression is not going on: six "broken marriages" among Babette and Jack alone, six or so children in their teens or pre-teens, siblings and parents intruding and exiting often unannounced, and not a psychiatrist anywhere in sight.

There is no feeling of trouble in Blacksmith – and that, of course, is what troubles Don DeLillo.

2

For the last hundred years or so, the divorce rate in the United States has risen precipitously in periodic cycles that have triggered public alarm. The publication of *White Noise* in 1985 came in the middle of the most recent of these cycles. From the mid-seventies onward, whether in panic over traditional values or hopeful of antibourgeois alternatives, academic writers have been proclaiming the "decline of the American family" and predicting its imminent "dissolution," reaching in the process uncharacteristically wide audiences.[3] "The decomposition of this bond is surely America's most urgent social problem," writes Allan Bloom in *The Closing of the American Mind*. "But nobody even tries to do anything about it. The Tide seems irresistible."[4] In *Haven in a Heartless World* (1977), Christopher Lasch suggests (more happily than most others) that "the present crisis of the family" might portend the massive social anarchy that conservative commentators have so long feared: "a drastic disorganization of all our institutions."[5] In *White Noise*, DeLillo takes it for granted that bonds of blood and marriage have been trivialized, and that in their trivialization society has lost one of its foundations: To that extent DeLillo echoes the strongest jeremiadic voices of our time. But it is in the dissent of *White Noise* ~jeremiah~ from the prevailing analysis of how the American family functions – where its "plight" originates, how actual families manage nevertheless to sustain themselves to the extent that they do, to what else is their operation allied – that DeLillo makes his strongest contribution to our understanding of suburban domesticity.

In *Haven in a Heartless World*, Lasch identifies what he and the sociological community take to be the major components of the family crisis – "'the sexual revolution,' the women's movement, and the decline of parental authority" – problems he traces back to the latter part of the nineteenth century.[6] Bloom reaches his crowning section, "Divorce," only after working his way through the same issues, and in roughly the same order, calling for a return of modesty, premarital chastity and marital fidelity, a renewal of reverence for gender distinctions, and an increased disciplining of the young at home.[7] For Bloom as well as Lasch, the outside world penetrates the sanctuary of the home and destroys its sense of purpose, seducing family members out of commonality into one or another form of soulless individualism – be it in the name of self-making or self-fulfillment, be it in practice more like competitive materialism or therapeutic narcissism. In light of the profound convergence of these diagnoses from thinkers at opposite ends of the spectrum, what is most fascinating about DeLillo's treatment of the multi-divorce family is how little he is interested in indicting the conventional trinity of demons or their godhead, the Imperial Self.

For all the divorces that mark the Gladneys, there is more than a touch of residual fifties mythology underneath their contemporaneity, plenty enough to keep the ghosts of Lasch's and Bloom's suspicions at bay. Father works, mother stays at home. Four normal kids, a station wagon, and a nice house on a quiet street in a small town that is the suburb of nowhere. Jack chairs the department of Hitler studies at the College-on-the-Hill, which allows him (like a fifties "sitcom dad" and many a real one as well) to reap the rewards and wrestle with the challenges of a professional life and still spend a great deal of time at home (often during the day). Babette "gathers and tends the children, teaches a course in an adult education program, belongs to a group of volunteers who read to the blind" – like a fifties sitcom Mom, a homemaker with minor outside interests for sanity and enrichment. For all the precocity of the kids, Jack and Babette manage to enforce house rules (Denise runs the trash compactor, Steffie relines the wastepaper baskets); they command allegiance when proposing group agendas, such as watching the sunset or going shopping; and they are able to solicit the children's good will in, say, welcoming Murray into quasi-family status or in joining Pardee (even Heinrich goes along) at the Wagon Wheel for dinner. Each of the children is capable of taking initiative: Denise is the first to identify her mother's secretive use of the mysterious drug Dylar; Steffie helps her dad prepare for his opening address at the Hitler conference; and Heinrich becomes a leader both of family and community during the waste-chemical accident.

The Gladneys are a representative contemporary family: What their contemporaneity consists of is a relatively efficacious, even compelling domesticity under which lies a basis of quicksand, the no-fault-no-shame divorce. Although both Bloom and Lasch in their own ways claim to be indicting forces that predate recent events, it is DeLillo who, for me, moves fully beyond the indictment of the me-generation that emerged in the late seventies and early eighties. And this is because DeLillo, in a way that Lasch and especially Bloom do not, has a feel for the way the colonization of the home by mass culture achieves this effect of a "close-knit nuclear family" without the ties of marriage and blood that, at least theoretically, grounded such families.[8] In *White Noise*, DeLillo examines not so much the individuating force of consumer culture as its communalizing power. What he sees is how consumerism produces what we might call an aura of connectedness among individuals: an illusion of kinship, transiently functional but without either sustaining or restraining power, a stimulant that at the same time renders one unable to feel either the sacredness or the tyranny of the family bond.

Let me provide an introductory illustration, in which the dynamics of familial consumerism as a system are concentrated in an actual shopping trip by the family. In one of those huge warehouses that have come to replace the town hardware store, while the other members of the family have gone their separate ways, Jack encounters a colleague, Eric Massingale. Asking Jack not to take offense (and thereby betraying that he knows Jack will), Massingale tells him that, without the academic gown and heavy-framed dark-lensed glasses that he wears at the university, he looks "so harmless" – just "a big, harmless, aging, indistinct sort of guy." Although Jack *knows* he is "the false character" that follows his marketed image around, he still feels hurt by Massingale's comment: "The encounter put me in the mood to shop" (83). The point here is not Jack's ego-fragility but that shopping offers itself as a balm for the slings and arrows of the professional-managerial workplace. In the central image of Lasch's title, Jack should be running away from the heartless world of the market into the haven of domesticity. But Jack in fact takes what is now an utterly typical course: He searches out his family, both literally and figuratively, at the Mid-Village Mall.

Jack gathers Babette and the kids together for a daylong mall crawl, punctuated by at least two meals: "I began to grow in value and self-regard. I filled myself out, found new aspects of myself, located a person I'd forgotten existed" (84). Taken out of context, the rhetoric of renewal suggests the usual therapeutic targets – pride (especially male vanity), covetousness, gluttony. "I kept seeing myself *unexpectedly* in some reflecting surface" (83). Mirrors are there to induce the narcissism, but Jack's desire is structured differently. He doesn't describe what he buys; nor does he buy with either vision or purpose. "I shopped for its own sake, looking and touching, inspecting merchandise I had no intention of buying, then buying it" (84). The sense of fulfillment seems to lie in the spending of money, not the actual acquisition of goods. "I traded money for goods. The more money I spent, the less important it seemed. I was bigger than these sums. These sums poured

21

off my skin like so much rain. These sums in fact came back to me in the form of existential credit" (84).

Part of what lies at the bottom of Jack's urge to shop is a sense of disappointment in the supposed "community" of the university. A colleague has taken an obviously "lascivious" delight in deliberately offending another colleague at the spot where, professionally speaking, he is most vulnerable: his reputation. Crucial to the sense of renewal is a reaffirmation of goodwill and solidarity in the alternative community of the home. The shopping spree is less a matter of personal aggrandizement or ego massage than it is a ritual of concerted vision. We might suppose that the other members of the family would not be difficult to recruit under ordinary conditions, but in light of Jack's uncharacteristic urgency they all become feverishly excited. "My family gloried in the event. I was one of them, shopping, at last" (83). By shopping with his family, he becomes "one" with his family, which in turn achieves its "oneness" through the activity of shopping. "*We* moved from store to store, rejecting not only items in certain departments, not only entire departments but whole stores, mammoth corporations that did not strike *our* fancy for one reason or another. . . . *We* crossed from furniture to men's wear, walking through cosmetics. *Our* images appeared on mirrored columns, in glassware and chrome, on TV monitors in security rooms" (83–4; italics mine).

Not only is the integrity of the family as a unit celebrated here, but the structure of the family is regrounded in the actual business of consumption. "Babette and the kids [were] puzzled but excited by my desire to buy" (83). Some of the initial excitement may be for shopping per se, but a strong current within that fever is generated by Jack's willingness to sanction the transgression of traditional family boundaries: Fathers do not shop, young daughters are usually not in the position of instructing their fathers. The key to the magic of this transgression is that it is only a flirtation: Roles are not so much transcended as refigured within the consuming sphere. By the very "reckless abandon" with which he shops, he is able to participate in the familial enterprise without abandoning what marks him off as the father, which is that he still, finally, doesn't care what they actually purchase: "When I could not decide between two shirts, they encouraged me to buy both" (83).

22

Similarly, for all the acknowledgment of the girls' expertise, they are, after all, waiting on him. ("The two girls scouted ahead, spotting things they thought I might want or need, running back to get me, to clutch my arms, plead with me to follow" [83].) Central to the reconfiguration is Jack's proposal that the children pick out their Christmas presents from Santa now, despite the fact that it is only September and that they are in sight of one another.

The point of this exercise is not simply the vulgar commercialization of Christmas, but how the gift-giving procedure reestablishes hierarchies and identities within the family:

> I felt expansive, inclined to be sweepingly generous, and told the kids to pick out their Christmas gifts here and now. I gestured in what I felt was an expansive manner. I could tell they were impressed. They fanned out across the arena, each of them suddenly inclined to be private, shadowy, even secretive. Periodically one of them would return to register the name of an item with Babette, careful not to let the others know what it was. I myself was not to be bothered with tedious details. I was the benefactor, the one who dispenses gifts, bonuses, bribes, *baksheesh*. The children knew it was the nature of such things that I could not be expected to engage in technical discussions about the gifts themselves. We ate another meal. A band played live Muzak. (84)

Jack is the patriarch who dispenses not only the funds that make purchases possible but also, more crucially, approval of the children's desire to consume: a blessing of the gift-getting. It is only right and just that he not be bothered with details, thus preserving his official role of ultimate aloofness but also allowing him to savor (this is *his* secret) the anticipation of surprise Christmas morning. As maternal caretaker, Babette has no such luck: On intimate terms with each child, she is made immediately aware of their desires, playing traffic cop and reassuring them individually of the goodliness of their intentions, their selections. The children take the opportunity both to accept the bequests that subordinate them and to play with their individual identities (choosing their *own* gifts), not finally as an act of separation but as a responsibility to others (make your own gift an entertaining surprise *for* the others). In short, the mystery of how the Gladneys function is solved: In the marketplace, each knows his or her responsibilities, his or her privileges.

[handwritten marginal note: I thought it was a picture of greed...]

DeLillo ends the scene abruptly on a discordant note. "We drove home in silence. We went to our respective rooms, wishing to be alone" (84). The return to rooms is understandable as self-differentiation, the backlash against too much "togetherness." Whether they wrap their Christmas presents, put their other purchases immediately to use, carefully store away what is not immediately usable, we don't know. Whether anyone decides instead to throw his or her stuff into a closet (to be dealt with later), we don't know. Steffie watches television. For Jack and Babette, if not yet the children, I suspect there is a lingering disquiet, as if somewhere in their blood, still not yet framable as a question, is the specter of a doubt: What kind of kinship do we attain if the price of our connectedness is *only* money?

3

In the seminal criticism on television and postmodernity, the representation of the family in television has begun to be discussed persuasively. The question of how television works *within* the family has not moved much beyond extrapolations from the formal content.[9] DeLillo's fiction lies at the cutting edge of mass-culture theory because he struggles to imagine how television as a *medium* functions within the home as the foremost site for what sociologists call our "primary" social relations. As DeLillo envisions it, television menaces the home with an omnipresent temptation to substitute the communal experience of the image for the ties that no longer bind.

Murray Jay Siskind, an ex-sportswriter from New York City, is a visiting lecturer in the American Environments Department at the College-on-the-Hill, a colleague of Jack who wants "to do for Elvis" what Jack "has done for Hitler." As a participant-observer in the Gladney household, Murray says he has come to feel vindicated in an ongoing argument he has been having with his students at the university, which focuses on the inherent worth of television. "TV offers incredible amounts of psychic data," he proselytizes. "It opens ancient memories of world birth, it welcomes us into the grid, the network of little buzzing dots that make up the picture pattern." His students resist with equal conviction. For them, television is "worse than junk mail. Television is the death throes of human consciousness. . . . They're ashamed of their television past. They want to talk about movies" (51).

The students are identifying with both the antimodernization of culture critics since the turn of the century and the increasing tendency as the century has passed to treat film as a form of high modernism. According to Murray, his students are also rebelling *against* what we can safely take to have been their own childhoods, "exactly as an earlier generation turned against their parents and their country." Thus Murray's urgent plea to the students can be taken literally: "I tell them they have to look as children again" (50).[10]

While Murray contends that his students have rejected television, Jack listens intently, then returns to the subject. It is no coincidence that Murray has been taking notes in the Gladneys' home; and it is no coincidence that all of the Gladney children are under the age of fifteen. Heinrich, Denise, and Steffie are each thoroughly, unselfconsciously immersed: They vie for control over the TV set (which therefore moves from room to room); when not actually watching, they talk TV trivia of one sort or another (contributing to the family as "cradle of the world's misinformation"); above all, they murmur things like "Toyota Celica" in their dreams. "If our complaints have a focal point, it would have to be the TV set, where the outer torment lurks, causing fears and secret desires" (85). Jack's fingering of television reflects a modernist sense of alienation that is also, perhaps first and foremost, a parent's lament for his children; his rapt interest in Murray's students reflects a resparking of hope for their futures.

Both Jack and Babette fear the "narcotic undertow and eerie diseased brain-sucking power" of television. Babette has designed the principal strategy with which they try to defeat television's invasive presence, which is "de-glamorize" it as "wholesome domestic sport" (16). She has made it a rule to watch TV *en famille* on Friday nights. The evenings themselves tend to be disliked: Heinrich pouts, Jack fidgets in boredom and in anticipation of reading Hitler, Steffie irritates the others by her sentimentalism.

141 558

25

The children are made wary of group television sessions, especially preplanned, but are by no means discouraged from television itself.

At worst, the Friday night sessions backfire, for instance, on "the night of the catastrophes." Uncannily anticipating the rise of TV staples such as Geraldo Rivera, DeLillo portrays an evening in which the programming resembles the supermarket tabloid. The entire family is transfixed in grotesque voyeurism: "We were otherwise silent, watching houses slide into the ocean, whole villages crackle and ignite in a mass of advance lava. Every disaster made us wish for more, for something bigger, grander, more sweeping" (16). Beyond the ethical dimension of taking pleasure in the sufferings of others that attends this particular evening is a more general point about the nature of television's threat: the specter here of group addiction, fascistic cultism in and of the family. "Heinrich was not sullen. I was not bored. Steffie . . . appeared totally absorbed" (16). Killing the capacity for individual response, television unites families in an orgy of sensationalism that leaves its participants, like any powerful narcotic, thirsty (in this case, bloodthirsty) for more.

One evening, when Babette is teaching her posture class at a local church, the rest of the family discovers that her class is being broadcast on local access cable.[11] Compelled beyond volition, they gather around the television and watch Babette's instruction without raising the sound, a detail fraught with Platonic terror. "It was the picture that mattered" (104). Babette appears as if in a state of constant becoming – "endlessly being formed and reformed" – yet it is not her that is acting and reacting but, of course, a swarm of "electronic dots." The "Babette of electrons and photons" touches each of them ("her image was projected on our bodies, swam in us and through us"), like a physical commingling, a joining with her and a cojoining with each other under the aegis of her radiated presence. The rhetoric of light's physicality suggests that the screen's ultimate strategy is to destroy the distinction between flesh and image, re-presenting the image-in-all-its-fleshiness as the thing-in-itself. If the vehicle that generates perception is to replace the object perceived, then television can be said to seduce us with a major reconstruction of the nature of reality itself. Jack

reality

feels "a certain disquiet" as the kids grow flush with excitement. Murray is there, too, undifferentiated from the others except for taking notes.

"It was but wasn't her" (104). In his foreboding, Jack speaks out of a stubborn effort to preserve the distinction between Babette-in-the-flesh and Babette-as-image despite the fact that he feels and understands its narcotic allure. "I tried to tell myself it was only television – whatever that was, however it worked – and not some journey out of life or death, not some mysterious separation" (105). Each of the children responds with unselfconscious zest and the equally innocent assumption that the others are elated too. Throughout the novel, the children give themselves over whole-heartedly to energizing rituals of familial consumerism: the lunch of "crumpled tinfoil" and "shiny bags," the Christmas-in-September shopping spree at the Mid-Village Mall, the night of watching natural disasters on TV. For them, the unannounced appearance of Babette on TV raises familial consumerism to a higher power. They feel exhilaration in the crossing of the boundary between substance and illusion, between their actual mother and her mediated likeness. They participate in something like a secular Mass: What is circulated as the transcendent is Babette's image, made holy by the power of the medium, a postmodern communion of the commodified illusion.

"secular mass"

Daniel Aaron has written of DeLillo's crafted separation from his characters: "I think he does care about their ideas, although he is professedly indifferent to them as 'persons,' and he isn't always so detached as he claims to be."[12] Of course, it is DeLillo who has crafted this scene to push beyond Murray's seemingly *uncritical* celebration of the medium, and it is DeLillo who, in giving the scene its final wrinkles, in effect confirms Jack's uneasiness. When Denise decides at last to raise the volume of the TV, she gets "no sound, no voice, nothing," yielding a silence that even the children experience as frightening. "She turned to look at me, a moment of renewed confusion" (105). Of course, Jack could tell Denise and the others that it is only a problem with the transmission, but that does not address the fear that in making of Babette an image the media has robbed her of her inner self, a process that by their rapturous passivity they have approved, supported, exploited.

Heinrich, the technological wizard of the house and also the last to take the concerns of his fellow family members seriously, adjusts knobs to no avail; when he flips the tuning dial, sound booms out on the other channels, which the group finds only more disturbing. Again, one could tell them that obviously the trouble is back at the cable-television studio, surely an amateur operation prone to this sort of thing, but such doesn't allay the sense that it is their mother who has been lost, their appetite for her image that is under supernatural censure. "As we watched Babette finish the lesson, we were in a mood of odd misgiving" (105). DeLillo has, it seems to me, pulled the plug on the proceedings.

Although the children are shocked momentarily into sharing Jack's disquiet, at the close of the program "the two girls get excited" and await Babette's return, to complete the adventure by sharing it with her. Babette's projection has not been so spellbinding that the reappearance of the woman in the flesh, with experiences to relate and a capacity to listen, would be a disappointment; at least the girls are not going to be disappointed, though Heinrich is conspicuously absent from the sentence. What DeLillo understands the family to have negotiated is signified by Wilder, whose youthful innocence is meant to augur the next stage of human experience. Throughout the viewing, Wilder alone has remained calm, alone has acted as if nothing out of the ordinary has occurred: For in the naiveté that signifies the advance of postmodernity itself, Wilder has simply taken the image to be Babette. "The small boy remained at the TV set, within inches of the dark screen, crying softly, uncertainly, in low heaves and swells" (105). Wilder's anxiety that Babette has "disappeared" – which is in developmental terms merely the common experience of toddlers when adults are no longer in sight – signifies here the danger of television mediating all experience: One day the transmission lines will go down and leave us staring before a blank screen, perhaps infantilized, no doubt helpless without our image-fix. If the chapter had concluded with the reappearance of Babette, Jack might have left us with a sense that the danger has been averted and regeneration is at hand. Leaving us with Wilder's tears, he issues a warning that our acts of recovery against image narcosis may (one day soon) come too late.

Jack invests his hope — even if he is too intimidated to say so —
in the maturing of his children into "postpostmodernist" alienation. I take Jack to be gladdened by the fact that the children share
his "odd misgiving" when the volume cannot be raised, a sign for
him that he is not going crazy and that the kids may yet as they
grow older follow in the way of Murray's students. The signs have
to be gathered from scattered moments, acts, habits. Ritualistically
burning toast, young Steffie cuts a pungent swath in the buzz and
blur of household white noise — a defiant effort to stir the senses
that television has numbed, first for herself and then for the others.
Prone these days to wearing a dark green visor, Denise has since
early girlhood preserved and surrounded herself with similar com-
modity-relecs of her own past — "from cartoon clocks to werewolf
posters"; in a world of displacements, she rescues "remembering
objects" from the trash compactor of capitalism "as a way of fas-
tening herself to a life" (103). Finally, there is Heinrich's appetite
for science, particularly the sciences of the environment. One day
in the car, Heinrich tells his father that the weather is unknowable
without the confirming testimony of the weather personalities on
the radio. "You're so sure that's rain. How do you know it's not
sulfuric acid from factories across the river? How do you know it's
not fallout from a war in China?" (24). On the one hand, Heinrich
is behaving like any other precocious fourteen-year-old boy, what
my mother called being "disagreeable" (she meant it literally), and
what Jack calls taking a "critical-observer" position. On the other
hand, by his facetiousness (he knows it is really raining), and quite
unlike Murray and the other avatars of postmodernity, he both
distances himself from a medium that wills to displace his senses
with its word and counts the cost of consumer capitalism's march
to power in terms of chemical and nuclear fallout that would be no
(Friday) night's entertainment to undergo.

4

I have taken my title from a line of Allen Ginsberg. In "A Supermarket in California," Ginsberg, here a spiritual as well as ethnic
precursor of Murray Jay Siskind, commented eloquently and perhaps without precedent on how the task of food shopping (tradi-

tionally relegated to women) was becoming in middle America a peculiarly familial ritual:

> What peaches and what penumbras! Whole families shopping at night! Aisles full of husbands! Wives in the avocadoes, babies in the tomatoes![13]

To his wonder and alienation, Ginsberg finds whole families amid the fruits and vegetables; the echo of "wholesome" throughout his litany betrays not a little derision. Whereas DeLillo is every bit as aware as Ginsberg of who profits from the conducting of family business in the marketplace, and is himself not shy of the satirical expression of an aesthetic or political judgment, he writes not in 1955 at the height of self-congratulatory domestic rhetoric in the United States but from the low point, as he sees it, of familial integrity. If one is searching for signs of potential renewal, the strange market-rituals of American families compel closer inspection.

After the publication of *Libra*, DeLillo granted Anthony DeCurtis (writer and editor at *Rolling Stone*) a rare interview. In the published transcript, DeCurtis asks him about the apparent "fondness" in his writing "for what might be described as the trappings of suburban middle-class existence." DeLillo does not reply that he likes suburbia (although he carefully doesn't say he dislikes it either), but that a kind of magic occurs even there which has, he implies, heretofore escaped representation:

> I would call it a sense of the importance of daily life and of ordinary moments. In *White Noise,* in particular, I tried to find a kind of radiance in dailiness. Sometimes this radiance can be almost frightening. Other times it can be almost holy or sacred. Is it really there? Well, yes. You know, I don't believe as Murray Jay Siskind does in *White Noise* that the supermarket is a form of Tibetan Lamasery. But there is something there that we tend to miss . . . something extraordinary hovering just beyond our touch and just beyond our vision.[14]

DeLillo is not quite telling all he knows here. If *White Noise* is taken as our guide, then "dailiness" is for all intents and purposes a synonym for domesticity; and the "radiance" within temples of consumption reflects not so much the marketing of commodities per se as it does the energy of familial interaction that takes place there.

The radiance to which DeLillo testifies is reflected in the exhilaration of his writing about the Gladney shopping trips – relatively sustained stretches of narrative, in which the comedy is playful and inclusive rather than belittling, in which a sparkling quotidian naturalism takes over from the more precious invention that serves darker suspicions elsewhere, and in which the reader (at least this reader, who ordinarily hates to go to the supermarket) is grateful to DeLillo for having taken him along. François Happe, a French critic who cares about contemporary American writing, has compared the Gladney pursuits within the supermarket to the reflex mechanisms of Pavlov's dog, but calling the supermarket a site of cultural brainwashing in *White Noise* is, I think, just exactly wrong.[15] Unlike their other family activities, the Gladneys know full well what they are doing when they go to the supermarket.

Early in the novel, Jack Gladney tells us of a Tuesday (unspecified, to indicate a routine break from the routine) in which Steffie and Denise were ordered to evacuate their grade school for health reasons and stayed home for a week. He then announces that the family (less Heinrich) went to the supermarket together, which is the focus of the entire ensuing chapter and, by implication, was the highlight of Steffie and Denise's surprise week at home. Something more is going on than a breakdown in the division of labor or an illustration of how little there is to do in towns like Blacksmith. Entering the grocery store, they encounter Murray, who seems to have been hanging out there and who testifies to its hold over his imagination, which he expresses in characteristically vague psychomystical language: "This place recharges us spiritually, it prepares us, it's a gateway or pathway. Look how bright. It's full of psychic data" (37).

In his interview with DeCurtis, DeLillo attributes to Murray a comparison between the supermarket and a Tibetan lamasery; in the actual exegesis, Murray mentions reincarnation, Tibetan death rituals, out-of-the-body experiences, and UFO trips but not a lamasery, which is a retreat for Tibetan monks. DeLillo's emendation is instructive: Although family members are emphatically not of one gender or dedicated to the spiritual arts, still the supermarket is a mecca that permits a special concentration, an active attention to the business of being a family. "The large doors slide open, they close unbidden," observes Murray: "The place is sealed off, self-contained. It is timeless" (37–38). In the supermarket, paying vivid attention to one another, the Gladneys tackle problems, renew affections and commitments, and orchestrate change.

In one of the contrapuntal vignettes, Steffie takes her father's hand along the fruit bin – an especially auspicious place within the market – emboldening Jack, who thinks her hand-holding is a solicitation of paternal protection, to raise the question of Steffie's friendship with her stepsister Denise. Jack presumes that he is about to engage in an implicit barter: his blessings as father in exchange for some concessions by Steffie to family peace. In the frank father–daughter talk that ensues, reversing roles of speaker and spoken-to, Steffie reveals Denise has her own suspicions of Babette:

> "Did you tell Denise you were sorry?"
> "Maybe later," Steffie said. "Remind me."
> "She's a sweet girl and she wants to be your older sister and your friend if you'll let her."
> "I don't know about friend. She's a little bossy, don't you think?"
> "Aside from telling her you're sorry, be sure to give her back her *Physicians' Desk Reference.*"
> "She reads that thing all the time. Don't you think that's weird?"
> "At least she reads something."
> "Sure, lists of drugs and medicines. And do you know why?"
> "Why?"
> "Because she's trying to find out the side effects of the stuff that Baba uses."
> "What does Baba use?"
> "Don't ask me. Ask Denise."
> "How do you know she uses anything?"
> "Ask Denise."
> "Why don't I ask Baba?"
> "Ask Baba." (36–37)

Steffie's delicious sarcasm makes the conversation come alive as entertainment for us. Although her father has been prompted (by Babette, probably) to suspect her of intrafamilial insensitivity,

[handwritten margin note: going to the supermarket a spiritual experience]

32

Steffie is responding here, simultaneously, to Denise's preoccupations, Babette's seeming predicament, and Jack's seeming unawareness of Babette's predicament.

I find the reciprocal insight of Steffie and those whom she is observing (insights that operate across generations and bloodlines) to be acute, the exchange of information and affect elegant, and the interventions already implicit in the exchange more constructive than not. Even Steffie's apparent disclaiming of responsibility — "ask Denise," "ask Baba" — functions diplomatically, a pretense of partial ignorance that operates as a gentle face-saving stir to her father to take the action that she, as stepdaughter and stepsister, cannot. In effect, Steffie has conducted the caretaking role so efficiently and intelligently that one wonders if her taking of Jack's hand was not in fact a setup. Later Jack realizes: "Steffie was holding my hand in a way I'd come to realize, over a period of time, was not meant to be gently possessive, as I'd thought at first, but reassuring" (39).

[handwritten margin note: role reversal of parent + child]

The exchange between Jack and Steffie is but one moment in a crowded "supermarket event." Denise deserts her parents to join some friends who are skimming the mass-circulation paperbacks ("the books with shiny metallic print, raised letters, vivid illustrations of cult violence and windswept romance"). By responding with bemusement, Jack and the others make clear that Denise's gesture of independence has, as it were, the family seal of approval. At one point Wilder manages to toddle out of sight. In his tour de force description of the moment when Wilder is discovered missing, Jack illustrates how well he is capable of attending to Babette:

> [Babette] turned to stare in a way that suggested ten minutes had passed since she'd last seen him. Other looks, less pensive and less guilty, indicated greater time spans, deeper seas of inattention. Like: *"I didn't know whales were mammals."* The greater the time span, the blanker the look, the more dangerous the situation. It was as if guilt were a luxury she allowed herself only when the danger was minimal. (39)

The ensuing search has a bit of slapstick to it (the adults scurrying to the head of the aisles, peering down frantically). Yet it also anticipates the last chapter of the novel, when Wilder nearly gets

himself killed by tricycling across the expressway: which is argu-
ably a dramatization of spiritual renewal in a stricter sense, something like reawakening to the miracle of reproduced life itself.

Murray's presence in the supermarket is more than a device for
reflecting on the action. The dazzling inventiveness of the talk
supports his claim for the energy that supermarkets can unleash
while relaying not an insignificant charge to those around him.
The immediate audience to Murray's exuberance is Babette,
whose effortless unconventional sexuality Murray finds appealing
and has said as much, in mutual appreciation, to Jack: "She has
important hair." "I hope you appreciate that woman." "Because a
woman like that doesn't just happen" (19). So, too, Murray con-
ducts his spiel on grocery store reincarnation just within Jack's
earshot, making it a kind of double seduction that Jack and
Babette reciprocate and that also, concomitantly, recharges their
passion for one another. Murray asks the Gladneys to his house for
dinner, and Jack is pleased that Murray is going to stay in town for
another semester; by the end of their jaunt through the supermarket, it is clear that Murray has crossed an important threshold
in his incorporation into the confraternity. At the final purchase
point, Jack and Babette caress each other, not shyly, and whisper
promises for what is finally unsuitable before the breath mints and
nasal inhalers.

At the conclusion to an earlier grocery excursion, accompanied
only by Wilder, all Jack and Babette had that would account for
their feeling of elation was "the sheer plenitude" of "crowded
bags," but this time they have worked and played to the fullest.
Jack describes the kind of sublimity that occasionally settles upon
the Gladneys, what Murray calls their "special forms of consciousness": "It was these secondary levels of life, these extrasen-
sory flashes and floating nuances of being, these pockets of rapport
forming unexpectedly, that made me believe we were a magic act,
adults and children together, sharing unaccountable things" (34).
There is an epiphanic quality to each of the moments I have been
describing, and together these moments react exponentially to
form a grand pocket of rapport, as if the radiance that DeLillo
identifies with the supermarket has by dint of the family work

34

within the supermarket passed over and into the Gladney confraternity itself.

There is a vital converse to this observation, and it holds equally: If the Gladneys radiate, especially in the supermarket, it is not a matter of hocus-pocus. The kind of intercourse conducted in the market generates an effect of kinship that pushes beyond mere semblance to genuine warmth and mutual need. All the more tragic, then, that the family is periodically rendered asunder, its members forced to configure alternative households and to build connectedness anew. It is the failure of the Gladneys to marshal their own recognitions of the sacred and the necessary that, in the final analysis, most depresses DeLillo. In the long run, Jack and the others are willing to let their ever-changing domestic association only *seem* like a "magic act," with no one held accountable, despite their sightings, for those "unaccountable things."

In the fourth chapter of the novel, there is a conversation between Jack and Babette that highlights the ultimate (dis)service that the temples of consumer culture can render to the multi-divorce family:

> On our way home I said, "Bee wants to visit at Christmas. We can put her in with Steffie."
> "Do they know each other?"
> "They met at Disney World. It'll be all right."
> "When were you in Los Angeles?"
> "You mean Anaheim."
> "When were you in Anaheim?"
> "You mean Orlando. It's almost three years now."
> "Where was I?" she said. (15–16)

The cavalierness of the family relations are underscored several times: in that Bee and Steffie may never have met, in that Babette doesn't know whether they have in fact met, in that Babette needs to think twice before realizing that three years ago she was married not to Jack but to Wilder's father. Jack teases Babette about where the amusement park is to demonstrate that he is sufficiently involved in Disney, Inc.'s marketing schemes to know the difference between the original Disneyland and its souped-up Florida cousin Disney *World* – a confusion that neither Bee nor Steffie, as the advertising-saturated young, would ever make (whether or not they have been to either place). The final humor of the scene is dark, since it rests on the notion that for Bee and Steffie to have attended Disney World together is sufficient, in today's America, for them to know each other as kin.

Consumer capitalism brilliantly exploits the need for strengthening family bonds that it has itself, in part, destroyed: The logical extreme of this process is indicated here by DeLillo in shorthand. He does not bother to remind us that Disney World is no carnival for the underclasses, no fair for the local community, no animal farm for children but a national, *the* national, mecca for families. Marketed as a place for families, Disney World provides the opportunity to have the experience of "being family": for individuals to glow in the mirror of "relatedness" erected by the park, which in its internal construction as well as its advertising promotes the idea that you must be family if you are here together. I wonder if grocery stores, malls, even TV rooms that emanate such radiance do not convey something of a similar message. If for at least thirty years whole families have been shopping at night, perhaps we have reached the point where the market is a mini-Disney World, promising that to shop at night is to be a "whole" family.

NOTES

1. A leading scholar of American literature in Europe, Marc Chénetier, identifies "la banalization et la trivialisation de la connaissance" as a central concern of DeLillo, especially in *White Noise,* and he cites the board game Trivial Pursuit as evidence for the impoverishment of knowledge and its uses in the everyday life of the culture. Marc Chénetier, *Au-Delà du Soupçon: La Nouvelle Fiction Américaine de 1960 à Nos Jours* (Paris: Editions du Seuil, 1989), p. 184.
2. Thomas Pynchon, *V.* (Philadelphia: Lippincott, 1963).
3. As early as 1970, in a book too much forgotten, Philip Slater set the agenda for the critiques to follow: "Technological change, mobility, and the individualistic ethos combine to rupture the bonds that tie each individual to a family, a community, a kinship network, a geographical location." Philip Slater, *The Pursuit of Loneliness: American Culture at the Breaking Point* (Boston: Beacon, 1970), p. 7. Others that

followed in Slater's path would include: Sar A. Levitan, Richard S. Belous, and Frank Gallo, *What's Happening to the American Family? Tensions, Hopes, Realities* (Baltimore: Johns Hopkins University Press, 1981); Eleanor D. Macklin and Roger H. Rubin, eds., *Contemporary Families and Alternative Lifestyles* (Beverly Hills, Calif.: Sage, 1983); Amy Swerdlow, Renate Bridenthal, Joan Kelly, Phyllis Vine, *Families in Flux* (New York: The Feminist Press, 1989). Donald Popenoe, *Disturbing the Nest: Family Change and Decline in Modern Societies* (New York: Aldine de Gruyter, 1988) includes a chapter, "Family Decline: The Career of an Idea," pp. 11–42, that examines the history of the sociology of family crisis.

4. Allan Bloom, *The Closing of the American Mind* (New York: Simon & Schuster, 1987), p. 119.

5. Christopher Lasch, *Haven in a Heartless World: The Family Besieged* (New York: Basic, 1977), p. xiii.

6. Lasch, *Haven in a Heartless World*, p. iv.

7. Bloom, *Closing of the American Mind*, pp. 85, 102–7, 118–21.

8. In his yet more influential *The Culture of Narcissism*, Lasch fulfills what is only promised in *Haven in a Heartless World*, namely, to examine the destructive penetration of the home by "the apparatus of mass promotion" (*Haven*, xvii); but the ideology that mass promotion is said to promote is, once again, "the apotheosis of individualism," with its concomitant personality structure, narcissism. Christopher Lasch, *The Culture of Narcissism: American Life in an Age of Diminishing Expectations* (New York: Norton, 1979).

9. See, for instance, Tania Modleski, ed., *Studies in Entertainment: Critical Approaches to Mass Culture* (Bloomington: Indiana University Press, 1986); E. Ann Kaplan, *Around the Clock: Music Television, Postmodernism, and Consumer Culture* (New York: Methuen, 1987), ch. 5, pp. 89–142; George Lipsitz, *Time Passages: Collective Memory and American Popular Culture* (Minneapolis: University of Minnesota Press, 1990); and Donald Weber, "Imaging Ethnicity in Early Television," paper delivered at the American Studies Convention, Toronto, 1989.

10. For an insightful discussion of Murray's commentary on television, see John Frow, "The Last Things Before the Last: Notes on *White Noise*," *South Atlantic Quarterly* 89 (Spring 1990): 423–4.

11. In "*Libra* as Postmodern Critique," Frank Lentricchia identifies two scenes that are primal for DeLillo's imagination: in *Americana*, wherein a character quips that television "came over on the Mayflower," meaning that the manipulation of the American dream by advertising is now a central determinant of our culture; and in *White*

Noise, when Jack and Murray visit "the most photographed barn in America," a tourist "sight" the attraction of which is not the barn but the occasion to share in the photographing of the barn. The themes that emerge from these two primal scenes converge as the Gladneys watch Babette on TV, a scene tellingly placed at the very end of the first section. Frank Lentricchia, *"Libra* as Postmodern Critique," *South Atlantic Quarterly* 89 (Spring 1990): 431–5.

12. Daniel Aaron, "How to Read Don DeLillo," *South Atlantic Quarterly* 89 (Spring 1990): 311.
13. Allen Ginsberg, "A Supermarket in California," *Howl and Other Poems* (San Francisco: City Lights, 1959), pp. 29–30.
14. The *Rolling Stone* interview has been reissued: Anthony DeCurtis, "'An Outsider in This Society': An Interview with Don DeLillo," *South Atlantic Quarterly* 89 (Spring 1990): 300–1.
15. François Happe, "L'Amérique de Don DeLillo," *Europe* 68 (May 1990): 56.

3

"Adolf, We Hardly Knew You"

PAUL A. CANTOR

> after the plastic surgery, the
> guitar lessons, the war, hitler
> learns he can sing. high atop his
> pink palace, he wonders why he didn't
> think of this before. his fans are
> better, his outfits brighter, and the
> drugs are the best he's ever had. people
> love him. he still can't act, but hell,
> now he gets paid for walking funny.[1]
>
> – Keith Alley

1

ADOLF HITLER is no laughing matter. In a world where truth is now generally thought to be relative, Hitler often seems to stand as the lone remaining absolute: the incarnation of absolute evil. Even the most broad-minded tolerance for cultural diversity seems to stop short of embracing Nazi culture as a legitimate human possibility. Hitler has become an argument stopper: "You say all value is subjective: Does that mean we have no objective grounds for condemning what Hitler did at Auschwitz and Buchenwald?" In short, people who can agree on nothing else will join together in rejecting Hitler and all he stood for. To defend or admire Hitler is to risk removing oneself from the acceptable range of rational discourse and branding oneself as a dangerous extremist or an outright kook.

Don DeLillo is a disturbing writer, and nothing shows more clearly how disturbing he can be than his unconventional treatment of Hitler in *White Noise*. The novel centers on Jack Gladney, a professor who specializes in Hitler studies at a small college. What is so striking about the way Hitler is presented in the novel is its overall blandness. In Gladney's world, Hitler appears to be just another subject of academic discourse, arousing no special passions. Speaking of Hitler, Gladney says at one point: "It's not a question of good and evil" (63). In *White Noise,* Hitler does not seem to evoke the moral indignation and even metaphysical horror that have become our standard cultural response to the *Führer.* In fact, the whole idea of Hitler studies quickly becomes comic in DeLillo's portrayal, especially when he links it to the study of another twentieth-century giant, Elvis Presley.

Whatever one may ultimately conclude about DeLillo's treatment of Hitler, it is surprising that critics have generally not viewed it as at least a problem to begin with. Many discussions of *White Noise* do not so much as mention Hitler; most touch on the subject only in passing, seldom even noting the oddness of what DeLillo does with Hitler in the novel. The only critic I have found who chooses to make an issue of Hitler in *White Noise* is Bruce Bawer. In a generally negative assessment of the novelist's career, he writes: "Perhaps the most disturbing aspect of *White Noise* is Jack's fascination with Hitler."[2] Bawer is troubled by the way Hitler is in effect assimilated to the mainstream of Western culture in *White Noise:*

> DeLillo's offense, to my mind, is that he refuses to make distinctions. To him, as to Jack Gladney, the question of Hitler is simply "not a question of good and evil." Nor, it is clear, do moral distinctions enter into his appraisal of any human act. (41)

Bawer is obviously being hasty here in identifying DeLillo with one of his characters, and assuming that just because Hitler is not a moral issue for Jack Gladney, he is not one for his author. Nevertheless, Bawer is right to raise Hitler as an issue in discussing *White Noise.* The bland acceptance of DeLillo's treatment of Hitler in academic circles seems to mirror the very phenomenon *White Noise* portrays: a scholarly world so open-minded that it can now accommodate any subject without evidently blinking an eye. Bawer is also right to note that DeLillo's interest in Hitler is not confined to *White Noise.* Among his earlier works, *End Zone* contains a character named Hauptfuhrer, and *Great Jones Street* contains a rock group which assumes the original name of Hitler's father, Schicklgruber. DeLillo's most extensive treatment of Hitler occurs in *Running Dog,* a novel which deals with the search for a supposedly pornographic film of the *Führer* in his last days in his Berlin bunker. Clearly DeLillo is fascinated with the phenomenon of Hitler, and presumably believes that to understand the twentieth century, we must somehow come to terms with Hitler and Nazism. If we want to appreciate DeLillo's achievement fully, especially in *White Noise,* we must accordingly examine his portrayal of Hitler.

2

Before rushing like Bawer to condemn DeLillo for moral indifference to Nazism, we ought to recognize that *White Noise* is not itself an example of Hitler studies, but rather a novel which portrays a professor involved in Hitler studies. DeLillo may be trying to characterize the contemporary world by showing that such a phenomenon as Hitler studies has become possible in it. In fact, DeLillo could find no better example of the flattening-out of contemporary existence than the routinization of Hitler's charisma at the College-on-the-Hill. Like all of DeLillo's work, *White Noise* portrays postmodern America. Faced with an ideology of freedom and self-development, and swamped by an overabundance of material resources, DeLillo's Americans are set adrift in a sea of possibilities, which, being equally available, become equally valuable, or, what is the same thing, equally valueless.

In particular, this situation results in the distinctively postmodern attitude toward history as a kind of museum, or, better yet, a supermarket of human possibilities, where people are free to shop around for their values and identities. Modernism defined itself in opposition to previous history, rejecting movements such as Romanticism and Victorianism in the name of the new truths it claimed to have discovered. Modernism conceived of itself as coming at the end of history in the sense of its culmination, the privileged moment when traditional myths were shattered and the truth finally emerged once and for all. The modernist skyscraper, for example, starkly proclaims its truthfulness, scorning all previous architecture for failing to understand the principle that form follows function. As the heir to the modernist heritage, postmodernism finds itself forced to live in the posthistorical moment. No longer thinking of itself as advancing beyond previous movements or eras to some kind of authentic and definitive truth, post-

41

modernism adopts a new – one might say more tolerant – attitude toward history. History loses its linear thrust into the present and beyond, becoming instead a repository of equally available styles and ideas. Consider the typical postmodern building, with an Egyptian pyramid here, a Roman arch there, and a Renaissance portico somewhere else. This is the flattening out of history: removing the privilege from any particular historical moment and hence equalizing all historical possibilities.

DeLillo portrays this process most tellingly in the wide repertory of imagined sexual roles available to Jack and his wife, Babette. Looking for the stimulation of pornography, this postmodern couple can take their pick from everything history has to offer:

> I said, "Pick your century. Do you want to read about Etruscan slave girls, Georgian rakes? I think we have some literature on flagellation brothels. What about the Middle Ages? We have incubi and succubi. Nuns galore." (29)

The problem with this pornographic cornucopia is that it overwhelms Jack and Babette, draining the eroticism from their existence. From the way they endlessly talk about and analyze their love life, it is clear that they have become too self-conscious about sex. With all the imaginative possibilities open to him, Jack is finally reduced to the basest level of erotic stimulation:

> I decided on the twentieth century. I . . . went down the hall to [my son's] room to find a trashy magazine Babette might read from, the type that features letters from readers detailing their sexual experiences. This struck me as one of the few things the modern imagination has contributed to the history of erotic practices. There is a double fantasy at work in such letters. People write down imagined episodes and then see them published in a national magazine. Which is the greater stimulation? (30)

For DeLillo the twentieth century has characteristically added to the history of erotic practices not a new form of sexual act, but a new form of *recording* sexual acts. The self-reflexive and mediated quality of this erotic pleasure is what makes it postmodern. What stimulates people is reading their own fantasies printed by the national media.

Jack's statement, "I decided on the twentieth century," is particularly revealing. Postmodern man is so obsessed with his autono-

postmodernism is about control

my that he refuses to accept even his historical moment as a matter of fate. Rather it must become a matter of free choice, like one's job or one's hairstyle. Because the whole range of history seems to be open to Jack, he can claim not to have been born into the twentieth century but to have chosen it. The price one pays for this complete freedom in adopting one's role in life, however, is that it becomes merely a role. In *White Noise* the autonomous self becomes the inauthentic self. As this episode shows, the sexual identities of Jack and Babette dissolve into a sea of erotic possibilities. To gain the freedom they crave, they must transpose sex onto an imaginary plane, where their supposedly most private experience turns out to be mediated by the fantasies of others. Thus one of the central symbols in *White Noise* is the twentieth-century supermarket, as explained by Jack's colleague, Murray Jay Siskind:

> "Unpackaged meat, fresh bread," he went on. "Exotic fruits, rare cheeses. Products from twenty countries. It's like being at some crossroads of the ancient world, a Persian bazaar or boom town on the Tigris." (169)

Here is the postmodern situation in capsule: Everything, no matter how exotic or rare, is equally available, from all over the world, and indeed seemingly from all eras of history. Everything is neatly arranged, everything is labeled, and, presumably, everything has a price.

It is while strolling up and down the aisles of the vast supermarket of academic possibilities that Jack Gladney comes upon an item marked *Hitler* and thus discovers his life's work:

> I invented Hitler studies in North America in March of 1968. It was a cold bright day with intermittent winds out of the east. When I suggested to the chancellor that we might build a whole department around Hitler's life and work, he was quick to see the possibilities. It was an immediate and electrifying success. (4)

However German its subject, Gladney's department of Hitler studies is a characteristically *American* phenomenon. DeLillo stresses the initial arbitrariness of Gladney's choice of Hitler as the basis for his academic career, no matter how obsessive he may later become about the topic. To underline the inauthenticity of Gladney's commitment to Hitler studies, DeLillo points out that Jack does not

43

even know German and thus must fake his way through his career as a Hitler expert (31). Like a good businessman, Gladney comes up with the idea of Hitler studies as a clever gimmick at a specific moment in time, when no one else sees the potential in the enterprise. He merchandises the idea like a commercial product. His success has less to do with the intrinsic quality of the idea than with its novelty. Jack finds an open niche in the academic marketplace and exploits it to the fullest.

Once a horrifying phenomenon like Hitler can be represented, it can be stripped of its aura and turned into a commodity. DeLillo shows this process concretely in *Running Dog*, where the putative film of Hitler becomes a hot item, sought after and bid for by a wide range of business interests. Gladney becomes the envy of his colleagues such as Siskind because of the skill with which he develops his Hitler line:

> You've established a wonderful thing here with Hitler. You created it, you nurtured it, you made it your own. Nobody on the faculty of any college or university in this part of the country can so much as utter the word Hitler without a nod in your direction. . . . He is now your Hitler, Gladney's Hitler. . . . The college is internationally known as a result of Hitler studies. . . . You've evolved an entire system around this figure. . . . I marvel at the effort. It was masterful, shrewd and stunningly preemptive. (11–12)

Jack's appropriation of Hitler follows familiar patterns of capitalist enterprise, including product promotion and consolidation of a territory. Hitler would seem to symbolize all the irrational and dangerous forces that have destabilized modern life, but for Gladney he provides the solid foundation of a successful career. When one of Gladney's former wives asks politely, "How is Hitler?" he replies: "Fine, solid, dependable" (89). This surprising transformation of the once willful tyrant into someone reliable is the result of the increasing familiarity and reproducibility of his image in the marketplace. Through the power of the media, representations of Hitler have proliferated and permeated every corner of twentieth-century life:

> "He was on again last night."
> "He's always on. We couldn't have television without him." (63)

Television brings Hitler into our homes and hence domesticates him, assimilating him into the mainstream of modern life.

Beyond the attenuation of the horror of Hitler that results from his achieving a kind of celebrity status in the media, DeLillo focuses on what happens to the *Führer* when the academic world gets its dessicated and dessicating hands on him. Along with Intermediate Calculus and Introductory French, Hitler enters the course catalogue in the form of the only class Chairman Gladney teaches:

> Advanced Nazism, three hours a week, restricted to qualified seniors, a course of study designed to cultivate historical perspective, theoretical rigor and mature insight into the continuing mass appeal of fascist tyranny, with special emphasis on parades, rallies and uniforms, three credits, written reports. (25)

As always the brilliant parodist, DeLillo captures perfectly the style of college catalogues, which can turn the most exciting subject into something prosaic and banal. Absorbed into the academic world, what many consider to be the most frightening reality of twentieth-century life contracts in scope ("three hours a week, restricted to qualified seniors") and becomes a matter of routine ("three credits, written reports"). The sober course description actually contains a bombshell when it speaks of the *continuing* mass appeal of fascist tyranny, suggesting that the phenomenon of Hitler has not been successfully suppressed and contained. But buried as it is in a course catalogue, this revelation loses all its force, soon to become the subject of term papers rather than of public alarm.

The culmination of the marketing of the *Führer* in *White Noise* is the academic equivalent of a trade show, the Hitler conference Gladney organizes:

> Three days of lectures, workshops and panels. Hitler scholars from seventeen states and nine foreign countries. Actual Germans would be in attendance. (33)

DeLillo is aware of how all-pervasive the ethos of capitalism has become in America. Even academic language is infected by the hucksterism of the advertising world. The advance billing of the conference only underlines the absurdity of trying to capture the enormity of the phenomenon of Hitler within the confines of "three days of lectures, workshops and panels." The international makeup of the conference reflects the characteristic cosmopolitanism of the postmodern world, in which the distinctive meaning of Hitler as a national phenomenon – it was after all *National Socialism* – threatens to dissolve. On the face of it, the idea of coming to a random small town in the United States in order to study Hitler seems ridiculous. Only the promise of "actual Germans" in attendance seems to offer any hope of authenticity in the conference.

But the conference proves to be a meaningless affair, failing to confront the seriousness of Hitler in any way. Like most academic conferences, it turns out to be largely a diversion for the participants, a kind of vacation:

> About ninety Hitler scholars would spend the three days of the conference attending lectures, appearing on panels, going to movies. They would wander the campus with their names lettered in gothic type on laminated tags pinned to their lapels. They would exchange Hitler gossip, spread the usual sensational rumors about the last days in the *führerbunker.* (273–4)

Hitler has become all too familiar to these scholars, reduced to the level of a mere subject of gossip. DeLillo's satire is right on target. The name tags with the gothic lettering are the perfect touch of academic kitsch in the scene. The cosmopolitan cast of characters only serves to highlight how national differences have been flattened out in the postmodern world: "It was interesting to see how closely they resembled each other despite the wide diversity of national and regional backgrounds" (274). Although Gladney feels even more inauthentic than usual in the presence of the "actual Germans," it turns out that they are no more capable than he of responding to the Nazi phenomenon with any depth: "They told Hitler jokes and played pinochle" (274).

The density of satiric detail in passages such as this suggests, contrary to Bawer, that DeLillo is distanced from the attitude of his characters toward Hitler. For DeLillo the academic treatment of Hitler becomes emblematic of a larger cultural problem. Any attempt to articulate the horror of a phenomenon like Hitler must inevitably fall short of the mark, and, what is worse, risks draining the horror by assimilating it into familiar categories. Given their distinctive habits, academics are in fact the least capable of coming to terms with Hitler and Nazism. Scholars hate to deal with or even acknowledge the unique; they always want to lump phenomena together under categories, to find continuity where others see discontinuity, in short, to place phenomena in "traditions." By setting *White Noise* within the academic world, DeLillo may have taken us close to the bloodless heart of postmodernism. What I have been calling the distinctively postmodern attitude toward history is, *mutatis mutandis,* a characteristically scholarly attitude: that all periods of history are equally valuable and worthy of study. It is a curious fact that postmodernism as a cultural phenomenon has coincided with the era in which the university has come to play an increasingly dominant role in cultural life, as a patron, an arbiter of taste, and an interpreter of meaning to the general public. Far from wholly identifying with professors like Jack Gladney, DeLillo may be using *White Noise* to suggest how the academic world, with its inability to deal with phenomena like Hitler authentically, has contributed to what might be called the postmodernization of contemporary life.

3

One could thus defuse the criticism of Bawer with the argument that the idea of Hitler studies in *White Noise* is only DeLillo's measure of the power of the alliance of the media and the academy in the postmodern world to trivialize even the most significant of historical phenomena. But this approach runs the risk of trivializing *White Noise*, making it tame and thus draining it of its power to disturb. DeLillo may play Hitler for laughs in *White Noise*, but he takes him seriously as well. Hitler is so potent a reality that even all the forces of the postmodern world cannot wholly drain him of his frightening aura. That, in fact, is why Gladney becomes obsessed with Hitler. In a world "full of abandoned meanings" (184), Gladney is searching for someone who can restore significance and value to his life, and the powerful image of Hitler offers fullness to his emptiness. As Siskind explains to Jack:

47

"Helpless and fearful people are drawn to magical figures, mythic figures, epic men who intimidate and darkly loom."
"You're talking about Hitler, I take it."
"Some people are larger than life. Hitler is larger than death. You thought he would protect you. . . . 'Submerge me,' you said. 'Absorb my fear.' On one level you wanted to conceal yourself in Hitler and his works. On another level you wanted to use him to grow in significance and strength." (287)

DeLillo is not a participant in the Hitler phenomenon, but its pathologist. In Jack's comic — because halfhearted, academic, and postmodern — way, he repeats the tragedy of Weimar Germany. DeLillo understands the psychological appeal of totalitarianism. When people lose their traditional bearings in life, especially religious guidance, they are wide open to the power of anyone who appears to have the conviction and self-assurance to lead them and thus restore meaning to their lives. DeLillo has a chilling sense that in the twentieth century only the criminals have the courage of their convictions. That is why one of the characters in *Running Dog* admires the Mafia:

"Who are the only ones who believe in what they're doing? The only ones who aren't constantly adjusting, constantly wavering — this way, that way. . . ."
"The families," she said.
"They're serious. They're totally committed. The only ones. They see clearly, *bullseye*, straight ahead. They know what they belong to. They don't question the premise."[3]

Uninfected by modern or postmodern doubts, the Mafiosi are still capable of genuine commitment and hence can recapture something of "Renaissance glory" (218). Like Thomas Mann in his analysis of fascism in his story "Mario and the Magician," DeLillo grasps the power of the man with a single-minded will in a world of individuals who have lost the ability to will.

It is significant that DeLillo refers to the Mafia in *Running Dog* as "the families." One of the keys to its power is its organization into families, a structure that is absent in the diffuse, anarchic, postmodern family at the center of *White Noise*. DeLillo is aware of the component of group psychology in the psychology of fascism. When people seek meaning in a totalitarian leader, they are seeking *communal* meaning, a restoration of their sense of belonging to a meaningful group. Gladney's course centers on the group psychology of fascism:

> Every semester I [showed] propaganda films, scenes shot at party congresses, outtakes from mystical epics featuring parades of gymnasts and mountaineers. . . . Crowd scenes predominated. Ranks of thousands of flagbearers arrayed before columns of frozen light, a hundred and thirty anti-aircraft searchlights aimed straight up – a scene that revealed a geometric longing, the formal notation of some powerful mass desire. (25–6)

The Nazis understood the importance of myth and ritual in building up a will to community and a communal will. They reveal the other side of the media in the twentieth century. DeLillo shows how media representations may dissipate the force of a phenomenon like Hitler, but he also suggests how Hitler himself was able to use the media to build his power. This passage dwells on Nazism as a theatrical force. The key to the Nazis' political success was their ability to stage their meetings, especially for the film cameras.

This passage also suggests why Gladney speaks of the *continuing* mass appeal of fascist tyranny. DeLillo suggests that the spiritual void that made Hitler's rise to power possible is still with us, perhaps exacerbated by the forces at work in postmodern culture. What we learn about Nazism in the course of *White Noise* casts the seemingly innocent opening of the novel in a sinister light. In a scene familiar to all college teachers, DeLillo pictures the mass arrival of parents dropping off their children at school at the beginning of the fall semester:

> This assembly of station wagons, as much as anything they might do in the course of the year, more than formal liturgies or laws, tells the parents they are a collection of the like-minded and the spiritually akin, a people, a nation. (3–4)

With tongue in cheek, DeLillo suggests how attenuated America has become as a community, how little holds it together as a nation. Americans are no longer united by a common religion ("liturgies") or even by political forces ("laws"). All they have to unite them is a common culture, reflected in this communal rite-of-passage, but this common culture is itself highly attenuated, less a matter of values and beliefs than of what are usually called "life-styles":

> The parents stand sun-dazed near their automobiles, seeing images of themselves in every direction. The conscientious suntans. . . . They feel a sense of renewal, of communal recognition. The women crisp and alert, in diet trim. (3)

These people do have something in common, but it is something superficial, a look, the image of sun-tanned athleticism cultivated in soft drink commercials.

In *White Noise*, DeLillo views community as something that has become deeply problematic. The problem is clearest in the Gladney family, which can find little in common except watching television. Family solidarity is threatened in the contemporary world because it rests on a form of myth, a kind of error undermined by all the forces for enlightenment at work today. Gladney argues with Siskind over the claim that "the family is the cradle of the world's misinformation":

> I tell Murray that ignorance and confusion can't possibly be the driving forces behind family solidarity. . . . He asks me why the strongest family units exist in the least developed societies. . . . Magic and superstition become entrenched as the powerful orthodoxy of the clan. The family is strongest where objective reality is most likely to be misinterpreted. (81–2)

Here is the dilemma *White Noise* poses: One can have community, but only if it is rooted in myth or error; if one wants truth and rationality, one will have to pay for it in the form of widespread anomie and rootlessness.

It is thus the atavistic character of Nazism that DeLillo sees as responsible for its hold over masses of people. Though fully willing and able to exploit the technological resources of the modern media, Nazism is in some sense a turn against modernity, tapping into the primitive strata of the psyches of its followers. Precisely because Nazism is irrational, because it rejects the Enlightenment, it fills a need in a modern society that has lost its cohesiveness as rational inquiry undermines the mythic basis of communal solidarity. Gladney sees a quasi-religious dimension to Hitler's power and mystique: He "spoke to people . . . as if the language came from some vastness beyond the world and he was simply the

50

medium of revelation" (72). Ultimately Gladney traces Hitler's hypnotic, erotic power over crowds to the fact that he filled a religious need in them:

> Many of those crowds were assembled in the name of death. . . . They were there to see pyres and flaming wheels, thousands of flags dipped in salute, thousands of uniformed mourners. . . . Crowds came to form a shield against their own dying. . . . To break off from the crowd is to risk death as an individual, to face dying alone. (73)

In this view, Nazism is the modern substitute for religion, using theatrical techniques to re-create and recapture the power of ancient ritual to give people a sense of participating in something larger than their individual selves and thus overcoming their fear of death.

Right after this lecture, in one of the most disturbing moments in *White Noise*, Jack reveals that he and his colleague Murray have been participating in the very phenomenon they have been analyzing: mesmerizing an audience ("We all had an aura to maintain"). Jack's lecture on crowd psychology has itself produced a crowd: "People gathered round, students and staff, and in the wild din of half heard remarks and orbiting voices I realized we were now a crowd" (74).[4] Here is DeLillo's concrete evidence of the continuing mass appeal of fascist tyranny: Even a lecture about Hitler can have something of the effect of an actual speech of Hitler. However troubling they may be, DeLillo is concerned with showing parallels between German fascism and contemporary American culture. To be sure, at first sight the connection DeLillo establishes seems to be ridiculous: He pairs Hitler with Elvis Presley. The Hitler lecture I have been discussing is actually a dialogue between Gladney and Siskind, in which – each promoting his academic specialty – they offer parallels between the German dictator and the American rock star, chiefly focusing on their devotion to their respective mothers and their devotion to death.[5] As plausible as some of these parallels sound, even Gladney has his doubts about allowing his subject Hitler "to be associated with an infinitely lesser figure, a fellow who sat in La-Z-Boy chairs and shot out TVs" (73–4).

Still, DeLillo may be on to something. No matter how weird his fiction may become, reality has repeatedly found ways to outdo his imagination, as the Bhopal disaster exceeded the airborne toxic event in *White Noise*. In another case of life imitating art, the American music business has produced a would-be rock star named Elvis Hitler. The title track of his 1988 album with Restless Records is called "Berlin to Memphis." The record company promoted the album with a sticker saying, "The Twentieth Century's Two Greatest Overnight Sensations in One Band. It's Hell with a Pompadour."[6] Although this album could hardly be described as a success, overnight or otherwise, it does offer confirmation of DeLillo's point that somehow the mass appeal of the dictator and the rock star are alike. Both touch similar chords in their audiences, both are in fact performers in the age of mass media, both fill a void in the everyday lives of common people, both appeal to primitive emotions, both fascinate crowds by the image, and reality, of violence.[7]

DeLillo explores the rock star side of this equation in *Great Jones Street*, whose hero, Bucky Wunderlick, understands the way he appeals to the darkest fantasies of his public. Bucky's popularity rests on his ability to embody and express the primitive urges of his fans:

> Fame requires every kind of excess. . . . I mean danger, the edge of every void, the circumstances of one man imparting an erotic terror to the dreams of the republic. . . . Even if half-mad he is absorbed into the public's total madness.[8]

Although critics and interviewers try to humanize Wunderlick's music, he insists on his potential for brute violence: "What I'd like to do really is I'd like to injure people with my sound. Maybe actually kill some of them" (105). In *Great Jones Street*, DeLillo develops the intimate connection between the rock star and death (see especially p. 231). It is not just a matter of death as the ultimate marketing tool in moving a star's records off the shelves, a fact of the business epitomized when one wag remarked at the time of Elvis's demise: "Good career move." The death of the rock star becomes part of his legend, usually the crowning part. Like the beloved of a Renaissance sonneteer, only in death can the rock star pass into a world of pure imagination and hence truly become a myth.

Elvis has certainly become an American icon since his death, his image impressed on everything from lamps to bourbon bottles. His presence in American culture today is no doubt more pervasive than if he were still alive. As DeLillo is well aware, Elvis dominates supermarket tabloids as much as any living superstar, whether with rumors of his survival in some strange form or the sort of psychic prediction parodied in *White Noise:* "The ghost of Elvis Presley will be seen taking lonely walks at dawn around Graceland, his musical mansion" (145). Clearly Elvis has come to fill some kind of psychological and spiritual need in the American people, becoming in effect canonized and the object of quasi-religious worship, complete with pilgrimages to Graceland. The fact that, as DeLillo notes, Elvis is conventionally referred to as "the King" (64) suggests what his function in American culture is. In the midst of the postmodern flattening of distinctions, people need to look up to something, and their media celebrities become a debased version of an aristocracy they can worship.[9] The American Elvis cult is a postmodern simulacrum of the German Hitler cult. In the midst of a genuine economic and political crisis, the Germans turned to Hitler for their salvation. Not faced with problems of this magnitude, but still experiencing a spiritual void, Americans turn not to an actual political leader but to a purely artificial image of greatness, the celebrity. The *Führer* is dead, long live the King.

4

What are we to make of the initially bizarre but ultimately significant parallels between Hitler and Elvis in *White Noise?* My first thought was to invoke Marx's famous formula:

> Hegel remarks somewhere that all facts and personages of great importance in world history occur, as it were, twice. He forgot to add: the first time as tragedy, the second as farce.[10]

It seems at first plausible to regard Elvis as the farcical equivalent of the tragedy Hitler brought on Germany. DeLillo could be commenting on the differences between the first half of the twentieth century and the second. A serious eruption of mythic irrationalism and systematic violence in the authentic realm of politics is parodied by a mere representation of it in the life of a media celebrity, whose heroic deeds are confined to roles on the screen and who therefore exists largely as a mere image. Elvis's relation to Hitler would thus be another powerful emblem of the swerve to postmodernism in our era.

Or perhaps DeLillo is commenting on the difference between Europe and America. As the offshoot of Europe, America does seem destined to imitate its origin, often in diminished forms. In conceiving the relation of another former colony to its parent, Salman Rushdie parodies Marx's phrasing: "Europe repeats itself, in India, as farce."[11] In *The Satanic Verses*, Rushdie explores the relation between premodern authenticity (religion based on revelation) and postmodern inauthenticity (films about religious revelation). At one point his characters begin to live out a parody of the story of *Othello:*

> What follows is tragedy. —Or, at the least the echo of tragedy, the full-blooded original being unavailable to modern men and women, so it's said. —A burlesque for our degraded, imitative times, in which clowns re-enact what was first done by heroes and by kings.[12]

It is tempting to use this passage to characterize what happens in *White Noise* as well. Jack Gladney achieves a kind of superficial depth in his life by a process of *imitatio Adolphi*. Rejecting shallow American conventions, he seeks authenticity by giving his son the German name of Heinrich Gerhardt Gladney:

> I wanted to do something German. I felt a gesture was called for. . . . I thought it was forceful and impressive. . . . I wanted to shield him, make him unafraid. People were naming their children Kim, Kelly and Tracy. . . . There's something about German names, the German language, German *things*. I don't know what it is exactly. It's just there. In the middle of it all is Hitler, of course. (63)

If Jack sounds somewhat unsure of what the real value of German things is, we should remember that he is praising the German language as an outsider. At this point he still does not know how to speak it. When he finally addresses the Hitler conference in German, he is forced to reject what is distinctive about the magical language and seek out its common ground with ordinary English:

> I talked mainly about Hitler's mother, brother and dog. His dog's name was Wolf. The word is the same in English and German. Most

of the words I used in my address were the same or nearly the same in both languages. I'd spent days with the dictionary, compiling lists of such words. I made many references to Wolf, . . . a few to shoes and socks, a few to jazz, beer and baseball. Of course there was Hitler himself. I spoke the name often, hoping it would overpower my insecure sentence structure. (274)

In the end, Jack's attempt to become German stays on the merely verbal level; he cannot work himself into the deep structure of the language; he can never really become German; he is merely a postmodern simulacrum of a German.

But by comparing Hitler and Elvis is DeLillo really pointing to the notion of an authentic Nazi Germany versus an inauthentic postmodern America? The difficulty with this interpretation of *White Noise* is that Nazism in the novel is presented as itself imitative and hence inauthentic:

I told Murray that Albert Speer wanted to build structures that would decay gloriously, impressively, like Roman ruins. . . . He knew that Hitler would be in favor of anything that might astonish posterity. He did a drawing of a Reich structure that was to be built of special materials, allowing it to crumble romantically – a drawing of fallen walls, half columns furled in wisteria. (257–8)

We see here that the Nazis were themselves imitating a model of earlier greatness, namely, ancient Rome (a pattern even clearer in the Italian brand of fascism). Evoking the Romantic image of the ruin, Speer reveals the aesthetic side of Nazism, which turns out to be a *derivative* aesthetic. Speer's architectural proposal sounds curiously postmodern, along the lines of what is now called deconstructivism in architecture. DeLillo suggests how much of Nazism was a hollow facade: just for show.

I have been talking about Nazism as some kind of primeval phenomenon, an eruption of authentic barbarism in the twentieth century, which becomes inauthentic only in contemporary media representations. But, in fact, with all his emphasis on Nazi rallies, parades, and films, DeLillo suggests that Nazism is itself a simulacrum of greatness and nobility, more the product of Leni Riefenstahl's camera than the heroic deeds of Nietzschean *Übermenschen*.

DeLillo develops this view of Hitler and Nazism more fully in his earlier novel, *Running Dog*. Dealing as it does with the search for a supposedly pornographic film of Hitler − "the century's ultimate piece of decadence" (20) − this novel allows DeLillo to work out the connection between Nazism and the media. One of the characters says of Hitler:

> Movies were screened for him all the time in Berlin and Obersalzburg, sometimes two a day. Those Nazis had a thing for movies. They put everything on film. . . . Film was essential to the Nazi era. Myth, dreams, memory. He liked lewd movies too, according to some. Even Hollywood stuff, girls with legs. (52)

DeLillo emphasizes the staginess of Nazi culture:

> This is theatrical, the swastika banners, the floodlights. . . . You respond to the operatic quality, the great flames. (99)

Hitler is again viewed on the model of Presley: "Like a pop hero. Some modern rock 'n' roller" (147). DeLillo begins to blur the line between the real world and the film world in *Running Dog* when two of his characters go to see Charlie Chaplin in *The Great Dictator*. This cinematic representation of Hitler debunks his greatness by reducing him to the level of Chaplin's little tramp, with whom the great dictator is confused:

> *The barber, or neo-tramp, who is the dictator's lookalike, assumes command, more or less, and addresses the multitudes.*
> *A burlesque, an impersonation.* (61)

DeLillo gives us a postmodern scene: His characters sit in an audience watching Chaplin playing a character addressing an audience by imitating Chaplin's own imitation of Hitler, who is himself presented as playing to audiences throughout the film.

But DeLillo has one last turn of the postmodern screw saved for us. When the film of Hitler finally surfaces, it turns out to be not pornographic at all, but rather an innocent, "almost charming" (235) home movie, made by Eva Braun for the benefit of the children cooped up in the Berlin bunker at the end of the war. And when we see Hitler, he is clowning around, doing an imitation of Chaplin. This is the ultimate postmodern moment: the great dictator mimicking *The Great Dictator*.[13] The result may be "Hitler humanized" (237), but it is also a Hitler considerably reduced in stature, shown in fact as a broken and defeated man, a hollow shell. As with Presley, DeLillo begins to develop parallels between Chaplin and Hitler: "They were born the same week of the same month of the same year" (236). And which one had the original of *"the world's most famous moustache"*? (compare p. 60 with p. 235). As the film rolls on, we begin to understand Hitler as a derivative phenomenon: "he was a gifted mimic. He did imitations" (236). To complicate matters, DeLillo leaves open the question of the authenticity of the film; one of his characters wonders if it really is Hitler in the movie: "Not that I'm convinced it's him" (236). Still, the result is to diminish the aura of Hitler:

> I expected something hard-edged. Something dark and potent. The madness at the end. The perversions, the sex. Look, he's twirling the cane. A disaster. (237)

In *Running Dog* the ultimate judgment passed on the Nazis is a postmodern twist on the standard condemnation: "That whole bunch, they were movie-mad" (237).[14]

DeLillo certainly ends up cutting Hitler down to size in *Running Dog*, debunking the myth of Nazi grandeur, but does he also end up trivializing Hitler, just as the professors in *White Noise* do? How could the feeble old man shown in *Running Dog* have been responsible for all the atrocities committed by the Nazi regime? To be sure, DeLillo may wish us to be aware that this is Hitler at the end of his career, thereby leaving open the possibility that at earlier stages he was the dark force he is usually thought to be. But still the result of DeLillo's choosing to portray just this moment in Hitler's life is, as one of his characters says, to humanize him. Although Bawer's judgment on DeLillo is far too simplistic, there is some truth in it:

> Jack and Murray compare notes on their respective scholarly subjects, Hitler and Elvis, and discover that the two men were really very much alike. DeLillo's point, throughout, is unmistakable: Hitler was just like us. We are all Hitler. (40)

DeLillo's point is hardly unmistakable;[15] as I have tried to show, his view of Hitler is extremely complicated and subtle. Nevertheless, it is troublesome that at some points DeLillo tends to efface distinctions that elsewhere he appears to take seriously.

I began by arguing that DeLillo uses the example of Hitler to show how in postmodern culture an authentic horror can become attenuated in representations of it in the media and the academy. This suggests a significant contrast between the world of Hitler and the contemporary world. But as DeLillo probes the sources of the Nazi regime's power, he sees at work forces that are similar to those he observes in American popular culture. The obsession with sex and violence in rock music is a response to the same spiritual vacuum that Nazi myth and ritual tried to fill. This suggests a significant parallel between the world of Hitler and the contemporary world. For both, the only hope of overcoming a paralyzing self-consciousness seems to be a dangerous return to barbarism. But when one examines DeLillo's portrayal of Nazism more fully and more closely, it seems that what it really has in common with contemporary popular culture is its inauthenticity. Both are forms of simulacrum: mediated and derivative imitations of prior images of greatness and power. Do we resemble the Nazis in their devotion to dark powers or in their theatrical phoniness? Is the world of Hitler a measure of our postmodernism, or is Hitler already a postmodern phenomenon?

I do not mean to suggest that DeLillo is confused about these issues. Rather, I find him fascinating because he embodies what I see as the dilemma of many serious authors today. I can express the problem in the form of this question: Is DeLillo a postmodern writer or is he a pathologist of postmodernism? I have tried to show that DeLillo is a powerful analyst and critic of those aspects of contemporary life that are usually labeled postmodern. His satiric techniques strongly suggest that he is distanced from what he is writing about. But in order to be a critic of postmodernism, DeLillo must delimit the phenomenon, above all, historically. To be able to call contemporary culture inauthentic, one ought to be able to contrast it with an earlier culture that was authentic. In this sense, Jack's father-in-law, Vernon Dickey, asks the key question in *White Noise*: "Were people this dumb before television?" (249). No matter how comic this question sounds, it raises an important issue: Can one point to concrete developments in the contemporary world that suggest a fundamental change in the human condition, such that we might speak of a new phase of history – the postmodern – or perhaps the end of history itself? Could one argue, for example, that the all-pervasiveness of television in the contemporary world has given a profoundly mediated quality to human life that it never had before?

With DeLillo's unerring sense for the texture and feel of contemporary life, he does much to suggest that we have indeed entered a new phase of human existence, with our televisions, our supermarkets, and our academicized culture. Part of DeLillo wants to say that we have lost touch with everything that was authentic in our world and in our culture. But I sense that part of DeLillo wants to say that nothing has really changed; things have always been this way. We have our television, but the Nazi Germans had their movies, and neither culture stood in an unmediated relation to reality. DeLillo is disturbed by the American present, but he is also deeply suspicious of any effort to romanticize a past. Hence Siskind's critique of nostalgia:

> Nostalgia is a product of dissatisfaction and rage. It's a settling of grievances between the present and the past. The more powerful the nostalgia, the closer you come to violence. War is the form nostalgia takes when men are hard-pressed to say something good about their country. (258)

DeLillo's choice of Nazi culture as the image of authenticity that fascinates Gladney seems at first surprising and even shocking, but not if one takes into account his deep doubts about any form of cultural nostalgia. I would argue that he chose Nazism as the subject of a romanticized past in *White Noise* in part to keep his readers distanced from his character's nostalgic impulses.

Near the end of *White Noise,* Gladney's cultural nostalgia is thwarted in another direction. Entering a Catholic hospital, Jack decides to turn from ersatz religion and look for the real thing:

> I said to my nun, "What does the Church say about heaven today? Is it still the old heaven, like that, in the sky?"
> She turned to glance at the picture.
> "Do you think we are stupid?" she said. (317)

religion

To his shock, Jack discovers that the nun does not believe in Catholic dogma. She merely gives the appearance of believing for the

sake of those who need not religious faith but the faith that someone else is still genuinely religious. The nun has devoted her life to
"the others who spend their lives believing that *we* still believe"
(318). DeLillo gives us another perfect postmodern moment: a nun
who is a simulacrum of religious faith. This scene shows DeLillo's
inability to keep postmodernism delimited. As its name indicates,
postmodernism must be defined in contrast to something else,
what came before it. But like many others today, DeLillo keeps
wanting to extend the range of postmodernism, above all to keep
pushing it farther and farther back into the past, until it threatens
to lose all meaning as a distinctive term. This process seems to be
the logical outcome of the very concept of postmodernism. If postmodernism is the obliteration of all meaningful distinctions, then
in the end it must efface even the distinction between postmodernism and any earlier phase of history.

Consider the moment when Gladney, reading obituaries, wonders whether the great heroic despots of the past – Genghis Khan,
Suleiman the Magnificent – thought differently about death than
contemporary men:

> It's hard to imagine these men feeling sad about death. Attila the
> Hun died young. He was still in his forties. Did he feel sorry for
> himself, succumb to self-pity and depression? He was the King of
> the Huns, the Invader of Europe, the Scourge of God. I want to
> believe he lay in his tent, wrapped in animal skins, as in some
> internationally financed movie epic, and said brave cruel things to
> his aides and retainers. No weakening of the spirit. (99)

Here is Jack's cultural nostalgia at work again. As with his fascination with Hitler, he is attracted to the barbaric Attila because he
wants to believe in an authentic form of hero, free of his own fear
of death. But DeLillo shows that Jack's fantasy of Attila is mediated
by the cinema: Gladney can picture him only as portrayed "in
some internationally financed movie epic." Once again in DeLillo,
where we finally expect to find the primitive and the authentic, we
get only the postmodern simulacrum, Attila the Hun as movie
mogul.[16]

This passage suggests what I mean by saying that DeLillo wavers
between criticizing postmodernism and practicing it. Gladney's vision of Attila could be another one of DeLillo's attempts to charac-

terize the postmodern condition, showing how it cuts people off
not just from the world of nature but from the authentic human
past, as they cannot help assimilating figures out of history to the
mediated patterns of their own attenuated existence. But, as we
have seen, DeLillo risks the same result in the way he chooses to
portray a figure like Hitler. DeLillo himself seems unable to break
out of the postmodern circle and offer a convincing alternative to
its diminished reality. In short, he can give us a vision of the
inauthentic but not, it seems, of the authentic. DeLillo is sufficiently distanced from postmodern existence to want to be able to
criticize it, but sufficiently implicated in it to have a hard time
finding an Archimedean point from which to do the criticizing.
That is why he disturbs critics like Bawer with his unwillingness to
take straightforward stands, even against the evil of Hitler. But that
is also the reason why DeLillo is one of the representative writers of
our age and one of the most illuminating. Even as he shares in the
uncertainties and confusions of postmodernism, he helps to place
it in historical perspective and give us some idea of how we got to
the point where in our day the "imperial self" is born "out of some
tabloid aspiration" (268).

[margin annotation: DeLillo offers no solution to post-modernism]

NOTES

1. The opening stanza of "elvis hitler, jesus satan, and the lazy boys,"
   Virginia Literary Review (Spring 1990).
2. "Don DeLillo's America," *New Criterion* 3 (1985): 40.
3. *Running Dog* (New York: Knopf, 1978), p. 220.
4. See Tom LeClair, *In the Loop: Don DeLillo and the Systems Novel*
   (Urbana: University of Illinois Press, 1987), p. 218.
5. For a similarly bizarre set of parallels, this time between Lord Byron
   and Elvis, see Camille Paglia, *Sexual Personae: Art and Decadence from
   Nefertiti to Emily Dickinson* (New Haven, Conn.: Yale University Press,
   1990), pp. 361–2.
6. I am not making any of this up. For learning about the existence of
   Elvis Hitler, I am indebted to a fourteen-year-old named Frey
   Hoffman, who is just as intelligent and articulate as Heinrich Gladney.
   For tracing down the Elvis Hitler album, I wish to thank Elizabeth
   Hull and the record library of radio station WTJU in Charlottesville.

7. Cf. *Running Dog,* p. 151: "Fascinating, yes. An interesting word. From the Latin *fascinus.* An amulet shaped like a phallus. A word progressing from the same root as the word 'fascism.' "

8. *Great Jones Street* (Boston: Houghton Mifflin, 1973), p. 1.

9. Cf. Paglia, *Sexual Personae,* p. 361.

10. This is the opening of "The Eighteenth Brumaire of Louis Bonaparte." See Lewis Feuer, ed., *Marx and Engels: Basic Writings on Politics and Philosophy* (New York: Anchor Books, 1959), p. 320.

11. *Midnight's Children* (New York: Avon Books, 1982), p. 221.

12. *The Satanic Verses* (New York: Viking, 1988), p. 424.

13. See John Frow, *Marxism and Literary History* (Oxford: Basil Blackwell, 1986), pp. 145–6, and Robert Nadeau, *Readings from the New Book of Nature* (Amherst: University of Massachusetts Press, 1981), p. 180.

14. Curiously, DeLillo uses the same adjective, "movie-mad," of the professors in *White Noise* (9).

15. I for one doubt that DeLillo wishes to claim that "we are all Hitler," but he does seem to suggest in his novel *Players* that a people in some sense gets the leaders it deserves. Commenting on the excesses of governments, one of DeLillo's characters says: "They had too many fantasies. Right. But they were our fantasies, weren't they, ultimately? The whole assortment. Our leaders simply lived them out. Our elected representatives. It's fitting . . . and we were stone blind not to guess it. All we had to do was know our own dreams." See *Players* (New York: Knopf, 1977), p. 105.

16. See John Frow, "The Last Things Before the Last: Notes on *White Noise,*" *South Atlantic Quarterly* 89 (1990): 422. This essay contains an excellent discussion of the role of the simulacrum in *White Noise.*

4

Lust Removed from Nature

MICHAEL VALDEZ MOSES

Everywhere we remain unfree and chained to technology, whether we passionately affirm or deny it. But we are delivered over to it in the worst possible way when we regard it as something neutral; for this conception of it, to which today we particularly like to do homage, makes us utterly blind to the essence of technology.
—Martin Heidegger, "The Question Concerning Technology"

1

THE WORLD in which postmodern reality is taken to be the only "true" one is a product of technology, or of its essence. Of all contemporary American novelists, including Thomas Pynchon, Don DeLillo has most fully dramatized this state of affairs, given it its most detailed, expressive, and philosophically powerful representation. *White Noise* is DeLillo's exploration of an America in which technology has become not merely a pervasive and mortal threat to each of its citizens, but also, and more importantly, a deeply ingrained mode of existing and way of thinking that is the characteristic feature of the republic.

DeLillo is not the first to reflect upon the question of technology. In the work of Martin Heidegger one finds important antecedents to DeLillo's own novel speculations on the relationship between modern technology and postmodern political life. However, to acknowledge Heidegger's historical primacy or the trenchancy of his philosophic critique of technology is by no means to deny or ignore DeLillo's considerable independence and originality. It would be inappropriate to label DeLillo a Heideggerian as if this simplistic categorization somehow provided an adequate, much less complete account of America's most gifted contemporary novelist. And while it is nevertheless evident that DeLillo is familiar with Heidegger's thought, echoes of which can be found at various points throughout his writing, there seems little point in ransacking Heidegger's work for the sources of DeLillo's fiction.[1] A more productive enterprise would entail the comparative study of the works of these two figures in order to understand how they converge (and diverge) in suggestive ways on a number of interrelated issues: the essence of technology, the mutually reinforcing character of technology and consumer capitalism, the critique of the modern "world picture," the inauthenticity of contemporary existence, and the existential analysis of death.

DeLillo's most astute commentators are in general agreement that the America of *White Noise* is a fully postmodern one.[2] For DeLillo's characters, contemporary American "reality" has become completely mediated and artificial; theirs is a culture of comprehensive and seemingly total representation. Interspersed in DeLillo's novel, woven between passages of narrative and dialogue, we discover a litany of brand names, advertising slogans, the flotsam and jetsam of consumer culture: "Dacron, Orlon, Lycra Spandex," "MasterCard, Visa, American Express." DeLillo himself does not place these consumerist mantras in quotation marks, and he steadfastly refuses to identify their source. (It is clear that these incursions cannot be directly credited to Jack Gladney's narrative voice.) They are the "white noise" of postmodern America that envelops the Gladneys and the inhabitants of Blacksmith, "a dull and unlocatable roar, as of some form of swarming life just outside the range of human apprehension" (36). The culminating example of these subliminal intrusions comes late in the novel: "CABLE HEALTH, CABLE WEATHER, CABLE NEWS, CABLE NATURE" (231). This last example, with its hilarious concluding term, "CABLE NATURE," advertises in a dense aphoristic manner the underlying promise of postmodern culture: Nature is on tap, on cable, readily available to any American viewer who possesses access to subscriber television. The sequence promises a complete and godlike control of the human "environment"; health, weather, news, nature itself, all are at the disposal of the consumer. To be sure, what cable television actually provides is only a representation of health, weather, news, and nature. But this is DeLillo's point: It is precisely by way of technology reducing nature to a postmodern *simulacrum* (a copy with no original), "CABLE NATURE," that man assumes sovereignty over a reality that was once understood to transcend man himself. Formerly regarded as superhuman threat, guide, or order, nature ceases to exist except as a representation which man both produces and consumes. Heidegger's most general term for this technological approach to the world is *Ge-stell* or "Enframing." By means of Enframing, which is the essence of technology, nature is "revealed" to be at man's disposal, and in so doing is transformed into a *thing* which man chooses to consume at his convenience. Heidegger illustrates his thesis by reference to the construction of a hydroelectric plant set on the Rhine:

> In the context of the interlocking processes pertaining to the orderly disposition of electrical energy, even the Rhine itself appears as something at our command. The hydroelectric plant is not built into the Rhine River as was the old wooden bridge that joined bank with bank for hundreds of years. Rather the river is dammed up into the power plant. What the river is now, namely, a water power supplier, derives from out of the essence of the power station. . . . But, it will be replied, the Rhine is still a river in the landscape, is it not? Perhaps. But how? In no other way than as an object on call for inspection by a tour group ordered there by the vacation industry.[3]

The hydroelectric plant, like the Discovery Channel or "CABLE NATURE," reduces and transforms nature into what Heidegger refers to as "standing-reserve" (*Bestand*), or what DeLillo might call the consumable product of consumer culture. If it is possible to measure degrees of mediation, then DeLillo's postmodern America is more completely given over to Enframing than was Germany in 1949. It is no longer even necessary for organized tour groups to visit the Rhine; it is sufficient to turn on cable television; the Rhine is available at the touch of a remote control tuner. Advances in technology make possible the ever more abstract and comprehensive reduction of nature into calculable units of the "standing-reserve."

Postmodernism, modern technology, consumer capitalism. The interrelationship between these terms invites the suggestion that an anticapitalist alternative, the eco-socialism of the Greens or the more radical communism of the Marxists, might offer some form of relief, some respite from Enframing. But whatever his right-wing detractors might have mistakenly assumed to be the case, DeLillo, like Heidegger, seems wary of such alternatives.[4] For De-Lillo, even those groups within contemporary American society most attentive to the dangers of technological capitalism ultimately participate in a technological approach to the world. SIMUVAC, DeLillo's fictional organization devoted to the simulated evacuation and care of victims of industrial accidents, is itself another product of postmodern culture. Battling for state funds to keep their organization alive, the group makes use of the "airborne toxic event," a real technological disaster, as a model for their planned simulation. The absurdity of this bizarre reversal reveals that these organizations operate according to the same logic as do those cultural and economic forces they ostensibly oppose. The identity of the right, in the form of big business, and the left, in the form of environmental watch groups, stems from a fundamentally shared conception of nature as an *environment*. It is revealing that this is the preferred term because it suggests that both pro-business and pro-environment factions fundamentally conceive of nature as some *thing* to be managed and controlled. Whatever their differences on matters of public policy (they are considerable), the lumber industry and the Sierra Club do not regard nature as something inherently higher or more exalted than man. For both, the *environment* is in man's keeping and control, and it is *his* responsibility to administer it according to a modern scientific understanding of the world.

Nor do more extreme turns to leftist politics in any way challenge this common assumption. Marx after all insists that his is a scientific socialism and that the triumph of communism will take place as a result of the transfer of the means of production from private hands to society as a whole. For Marx, capitalism is a necessary preliminary stage on the way to socialism, one providing the means by which man frees himself from the tyranny of nature. The catastrophic environmental record of communist governments in this century simply confirms that Marxism merely transfers the power over nature from the individual to the society as a whole, without fundamentally altering or even questioning the modern scientific understanding of nature as that which must be made to serve man's needs. In this crucial respect it does not matter whether the nuclear reactors and industrial plants are controlled by private hands or by society as a whole. The by-products of "technology with a human face" (DeLillo's richly suggestive parody of Alexander Dubček's "socialism with a human face") – nuclear waste, chemical pollutants, airborne toxic events – are in any event as deadly to communists as to capitalists.

2

The technological understanding of the world, what Heidegger calls the "essence" of technology, is so deeply ingrained in the minds of DeLillo's characters that it comes to seem unremarkable, merely the necessary expression of the way things are. In an attempt to justify her use of the drug Dylar, Gladney's wife Babette offers the following interpretation of the world and the way in which it must necessarily be approached:

> You know how I am. I think everything is correctible. Given the right attitude and the proper effort, a person can change a harmful condition by reducing it to its simplest parts. You can make lists, invent categories, devise charts and graphs. This is how I am able to teach my students how to stand, sit and walk, even though I know you think these subjects are too obvious and nebulous and generalized to be reduced to component parts. I'm not a very ingenious person but I know how to break things down, how to separate and classify. We can analyze posture, we can analyze eating, drinking and even breathing. How else do you understand the world, is my way of looking at it. (191–2)

Although she is not aware of it, Babette echoes Bacon and Descartes in her approach to the most basic human problems and activities and in her understanding of the world. This rigorously reductive conception of even the most natural human activities is a rich source of amusement and satire in DeLillo's work. In an earlier novel more systematically devoted to the modern scientific project, *Ratner's Star*, a scientist named Evinrude (as in the outboard motor) laments that he has "never learned to run." He explains, "The subject of running is foreign to me. As a child I wasn't taught how to run and I've never been able to pick it up on my own. It's something I've always envied in other people, this marvelous ability to run."[5] Babette's pragmatic approach to life is only a more mundane version of Evinrude's theoretical amazement in the face of the natural. Evinrude represents a more exaggerated and grotesque example of that Cartesian dualism between subjective consciousness and objective extension that continues to play itself out in Babette's seminar on posture. Both Babette and Evinrude understand the world as a form of mechanics. There are no given or natural activities, only technical procedures by which consciousness learns to master its environment, an environment that includes the body. Babette's classes for the elderly of Blacksmith in such arcane and difficult subjects as posture, sitting, standing, and breathing are a comic version of the world rendered as pure *techne* (originally meaning in Greek the art of making or doing), if we take this term in its modern, post-Baconian sense.

DeLillo clearly intends his reader to regard training in sitting or running for the physically healthy as an absurdity. Nevertheless he suggests that the theory behind the seemingly insatiable appetite of Americans for self-help workshops, therapy sessions, and technical training in the quotidian stems from a generally unexamined premise of American life that Babette articulates: "everything is correctible." Innocuous enough on the surface, Babette's axiom is the very basis of the modern technological approach to the world, an approach more fully articulated by the postmodern savant Murray Jay Siskind, who tells Jack to put his "faith in technology":

> "It got you here, it can get you out. This is the whole point of technology. It creates an appetite for immortality on the one hand. It threatens universal extinction on the other. Technology is lust removed from nature. . . . It prolongs life, it provides new organs for those that wear out. New devices, new techniques every day. Lasers, masers, ultrasound. Give yourself up to it, Jack. Believe in it." (285)

→ technology requires belief (a sort of religion)

For every problem a solution. For every desire a technique. For every natural limitation a technological breakthrough. Immortality or lust removed from nature.

Like Heidegger, DeLillo provides a relatively precise historical origin for the modern technological understanding of the world: seventeenth-century Western Europe. (Heidegger's consistent critique of Cartesian metaphysics as the foundation of the modern technological understanding is well known.)[6] Whereas in *White*

Noise, DeLillo only obliquely suggests the sources for the American faith in technology, elsewhere in his fiction he is more explicit. *Ratner's Star* stands as DeLillo's contemporary version of Book III of Swift's *Gulliver's Travels*, bearing the same relationship to post-Einsteinian science as Swift's satire did to Baconian science.[7] The protagonist of the work, Billy Twillig, a fourteen-year-old *Wunderkind*, the first individual to win a Nobel prize for mathematics, recalls how it was that he was drawn to "a life fulfilled in mathematics and philosophy" (64). In a series of three dreams his Baconian vocation is announced to him: "The first two concerned the terror of nature not understood and the last of them harbored a poem that pointed a way to the tasks of science. The world was comprehensible, a plane of equations, all knowledge able to be welded, all nature controllable" (64). In the same scene in which Billy recalls his childhood dreams, his recollections are thematically connected to and temporally juxtaposed with the historical origins of modern science. LoQuadro, another scientist and acquaintance of Billy, lectures the protagonist: "Consider science itself. It used to be thought that the work of science would be completed in the very near future. This was, oh, the seventeenth century. It was just a matter of time before all knowledge was integrated and made available, all the inmost secrets pried open" (65). LoQuadro immediately explodes the dream that Billy shares with modern technological science: "This notion persisted for well over two hundred years. But the thing continues to expand. . . . It refuses to be contained. Every time we make a breakthrough we think this is it: the breakthrough. But the thing keeps pushing out. It breaks through the breakthrough" (65–6).

The frustration of modern science finds its more familiar contemporary echo in Babette's exchange with Jack over the ominously unsettling character of recombinant DNA, the technology employed to bring the airborne toxic event under control:

> "A cloud-eating microbe or whatever. There is just no end of surprise. All the amazement that's left in the world is microscopic. But I can live with that. What scares me is have they thought it through completely?"
> "You feel a vague foreboding," I said.
> "I feel they're working on the superstitious part of my nature. Every

advance is worse than the one before because it makes me more
scared."
"Scared of what?"
"The sky, the earth, I don't know."
"The greater the scientific advance, the more primitive the fear."
(161)

The seventeenth century is important for DeLillo for another
reason; it is the century in which, as Frank Lentricchia has pointed
out, the "invention" of television comes over to the New World on
the *Mayflower*.[8] Lentricchia suggests that for DeLillo the origins of
postmodern American "identity" lie in that projected ideal of selfhood which the pilgrims, fleeing the constraints of the Old World,
bring to the New World. Television, particularly in the form of
advertising, produces and then circulates that image of the self that
Americans, even before they arrived at Plymouth Rock, had
longed to become. One might say that for DeLillo the seventeenth
century is the one in which America is invented in the minds of
those Europeans who first settled in the New World. It is not too
farfetched to suggest that DeLillo connects the invention of television (the distinctive third person whom each American would like
to become), the invention of (postmodern) America, and the invention of the technological conception of the world. What all
have in common is the dream of entirely remaking the individual,
of freeing man from all natural constraints, of living in the brave
new world, or as Babette in a more prosaic vein would have it, a
world in which "everything is correctible." Babette's pragmatic
approach to life hints at the underlying connection between modern natural science and modern political science. For those founding fathers of the republic, who looked back to Locke and more
distantly to Hobbes to guide them, were among the great pioneers
who went in search of "new seas and unknown lands."[9] The new
science of nature furnished them with the tools necessary to construct the new science of man. And America was their laboratory.

3

Three Mile Island. Chernobyl. The Airborne Toxic Event. The more
vigorously man pursues the ultimate dream of modern techno-

logical science – the conquest of the final natural limit, death – the more rapidly that dream seems to recede and the more imminent seems the historically unprecedented nightmare that technology visits upon man. And yet, for DeLillo as for Heidegger, the danger of technology is greater on the metaphysical than on the physical level. At the very least, Jack and his family can *see* the airborne toxic event and can recognize in it a potential threat to their physical existence. But the most sinister and insidious aspect of modern technology is its more or less undetectable effect on the psyche. To put this in Heideggerian terms, technology tends to impose on man an inauthentic existence:

> The threat to man does not come in the first instance from the potentially lethal machines and apparatus of technology. The actual threat has already affected man in his essence. The rule of Enframing threatens man with the possibility that it could be denied to him . . . to experience the call of a more primal truth.[10]

For DeLillo's characters, the immediate threat of death, brought on in some cases by the apparent failures of technology, may paradoxically serve a potentially redeeming function. The far greater danger is that technology may succeed in creating an illusion that it constitutes the only possible manner by which human beings apprehend themselves and their relationship to the world. The chief lure of technology, and its principal technique for domination over man's "essence" (to use Heidegger's phrase) is its constantly reaffirmed promise of immortality.

In the postmodern world the prospect of immortality must seem oddly out of place. After all, is not postmodern society precisely the one which has become fully demystified and secularized? For DeLillo, however, postmodern reality unexpectedly produces its own set of myths, cults, gods, and immortals. The concluding passage of *White Noise* reveals the quintessential postmodern environment, the supermarket, to be completely saturated with the aura of the sacred:

> The terminals are equipped with holographic scanners, which decode the binary secret of every item, infallibly. This is the language of waves and radiation, or how the dead speak to the living. . . . Everything we need that is not food or love is here in the tabloid racks. The tales of the supernatural and the extraterrestrial. The

technology as
religion

miracle vitamins, the cures for cancer, the remedies for obesity. The cults of the famous and the dead. (326)

In dramatic fashion DeLillo illustrates for us what Horkheimer and Adorno termed the dialectic of enlightenment, the paradoxical way in which scientific enlightenment reverts to new forms of mythology.[11] The concluding passage from *White Noise* reveals that the sacred language, "how the dead speak to the living," is the mode of communication specific to technology, "the language of waves and radiation." But how is it that technology effects this new mystification? What is it in the nature of postmodern reality, besides the credulity of tabloid readers, that produces the "cults of the famous and the dead"? The answers would seem to lie in the increasingly nonreferential character of postmodern culture. Since the technological media — television, the tabloids, radio, cinema — ultimately create their own reality, they appear to be free from all natural contraints on their constructions. They possess the seemingly limitless power to transform and reconstitute the very being of the contemporary individual.

In a telling scene in the novel, Babette's image suddenly appears on the Gladneys' television. Jack wonders,

> Was she dead, missing, disembodied? Was this her spirit, her secret self, some two-dimensional facsimile released by the power of technology[?] If she was not dead, was I? . . . It was the picture that mattered, the face in black and white, animated but also flat, distanced, sealed off, timeless. It was but wasn't her. . . . Waves and radiation. Something leaked through the mesh. She was shining a light on us, she was *coming into being*. (104; italics mine)

No longer the merely mortal individual Jack had seen just fifteen minutes earlier, Babette has become a luminous presence, a being permanently enduring in a timeless state.

Babette's is just one among many ghosts, including those of John Wayne, Howard Hughes, and Elvis Presley, whose spirits haunt the postmodern world. A canny diagnostician of the postmodern sensibility, DeLillo clearly understands that for millions of his followers Elvis *is* a latter-day saint, and that it is the technological power of the media which effects his canonization, preserves his iconographic image, keeps him alive forever. The tre-

religion

Elvis as saint

mendous capacity of film to *animate* gives it the apparent power to immortalize those whom it enframes. To be sure, the media have a special hunger for death and destruction (the raison d'être of local televised news). But the technological media also guarantee an essential psychic and physical distance between viewer and event, while creating the illusion of intimacy and nearness.[12] So immense is this technological power that a character like Jack Gladney who finds himself in the path of the deadly toxic cloud almost involuntarily conceptualizes it as a colossal postmodern representation: "The cloud resembled a national promotion for death, a multimillion-dollar campaign backed by radio spots, heavy print and billboard, TV saturation" (158). The technological media thus alienate the individual from personal death in at least two ways. First, they transform the deaths of all individuals, insofar as they are captured on film or in "heavy print," into yet another commodity intended for mass consumption.[13] Second, by imposing an increasingly automatic and involuntary identification with the camera eye, the media fosters the illusion that the witnessing consciousness of the individual television viewer, like the media themselves, is a permanent fixture possessing a transcendental perspective.

Both of these technological capacities reinforce what Heidegger terms the inauthenticity of existence that characterizes the public "they" (*das Man*). By transforming death into a product which is eagerly consumed (the Gladneys never get enough of televised disasters), the media enormously reinforce and heighten the illusion that death happens only to others. When the toxic spill takes place not far from Jack's home, he initially ignores it, since life-threatening disasters, as the televised news represents them, always happen elsewhere, and principally, if not exclusively, affect the poor, not the bourgeoisie (119). Heidegger would locate this particular psychology of inauthentic being in its tendency to say "one dies," rather than "I die."[14] For Heidegger, this tendency is not something specific to technological society, but it is very much reinforced within it. DeLillo gives greater, or at least more explicit, emphasis to the economic forces at work. In a consumer culture, wealth provides the illusion of invulnerability. Speaking of the comfortably well-off parents of Jack's students, Babette says, "I

have trouble imagining death at that income level" (6). The power
of technology allows its possessor or user to cover over the nearness and inevitablity of personal death. The greater the wealth, the
greater the quantum of technological power, the more distant personal death seems.

The technology of modern medicine further reinforces this self-
alienated character of postmodern death. Even when Jack must
approach his own finitude more or less alone, outside of the
sphere of a public event or televised disaster, he discovers that his
"death" is not his own. By rendering "death" as a set of computer-
generated data and technologically reproducible representations of
the body, modern medical technology distances the dying individual from the intensely personal character of his mortality. As
Jack explains,

> You are said to be dying and yet are separate from the dying, can
> ponder it at your leisure, literally see on the X-ray photograph or
> computer screen the horrible alien logic of it all. It is when death is
> rendered graphically, is televised so to speak, that you sense an eerie
> separation between your condition and yourself. A network of sym-
> bols has been introduced, an entire awesome technology wrested
> from the gods. It makes you feel like a stranger in your own dying.
> (142)

The technology of the hospital functions as an extension of the
technology of the public media, of television.

The identification of the individual viewer with the camera eye
has its specific corollary in Heidegger's existential analysis of public
or clock time.[15] As opposed to the "temporality" of authentic
being, which must resolutely acknowledge that its "time" is personal and finite, directed toward its own death, clock time or
public time is a reification and impersonalization of temporality.
Clock time belongs to no one in particular. Time becomes an infinite series of quantifiable units – seconds, minutes, hours – each
mathematically equivalent unit interchangeable with every other
and equally available to all persons. For Heidegger, the incessant
attention to clock time diverts the individual away from finitude,
and threatens to strand authentic being (*Dasein*) in the fallen public world in which time is endless. The camera eye/I of postmodernity is the technological intensification of clock time. The con-

sciousness of the camera eye/I is permanent, omniscient, invulnerable, no matter how close to death it seems to approach. In the postmodern world in which CNN broadcasts twenty-four hours a day, seven days a week, fifty-two weeks a year, there is no dead air, only the illusion of an infinite horizon for consciousness.

4

The greatest threat of technology is its promise of immortality; its most Faustian form in *White Noise* is Dylar. The drug is a failure, but it is worthwhile to consider how it is that for DeLillo technology is most dangerous when it presents itself with "a human face." Dylar promises not to make man immortal, but rather to eliminate the individual's fear of death. Were it to succeed, it would annihilate that innate characteristic of *Dasein* to which the early Heidegger devoted so much philosophic analysis: *Angst*. Jack and Babette are filled with anxiety, a kind of nameless and objectless dread that may unexpectedly reveal itself as the fear of individual death. And it is this fear which drives Babette to Dylar. In the scene in which Jack confronts her, DeLillo gives (in effect) a comic rendition of the Heideggerian analysis of *Angst* and its relationship to inauthentic existence. In an amusing reversal of the Heideggerian formula, Jack asks, "How can you be sure it is death you fear? Death is so vague. . . . Maybe you just have a personal problem that surfaces in the form of a great universal subject. . . . There must be something else, an underlying problem" (196–7). Babette's response is the Heideggerian retort, "What could be more underlying than death?" (197). DeLillo illustrates the tendency of an individual like Jack to studiously avert his attention from his own finitude. Since *Angst* or fear of death is so vague, so objectless, it becomes possible for the inauthentic self to overcome its anxiety by focusing on a specific, and often trivial cause. Jack suggests to Babette that she is actually worried about her weight. Dylar promises to make Jack's rather crude strategies seem quaint, if not completely outmoded. The technological solution is psychobiological; synthesize pharmacological inhibitors that will block those receptors in the brain that respond to or produce the fear of death.

"Dylarama," the final section of *White Noise*, dramatizes the confrontation between Heidegger's existential understanding of human finitude and Bacon's scientifically reductive solution to the human fear of death. Although Dylar ultimately fails to deliver on the Baconian promise, it nevertheless proves itself the ultimate postmodern drug. Like its predecessor in *Great Jones Street* which denies to human beings the capacity of speech or logos, Dylar cannot be tested on animals. By their very nature as un-selfconscious and prelinguistic beings, animals remain unaffected by either of the drugs. And although both products promise the ultimate high, their effect, at least in theory, would be to return human beings to a blissful but subhuman state, free of either logos or the knowledge of personal finitude.[16] Dylar is peculiarly suited to a postmodern culture insofar as it makes no claims to treat causes, only to alleviate symptoms. The technocratic and behaviorist approach of Grey Research, the firm in *White Noise* that manufactures Dylar, follows the instrumental reasoning of a purely representational conception of the world; manipulate the signs, deconstruct the symptoms, and the cause or referent in effect disappears.

The grotesquely funny and violent scene in which Jack finally confronts Willie Mink (Mr. Grey) is a comic travesty of postmodern reality. An unfortunate side effect of Dylar renders its user incapable of distinguishing between words and things. When Jack says gently, "Hail of bullets," Mink hits the floor (311). Moreover, the huge doses of Dylar induce in Mink a psychotic state that makes him incapable of responding to Jack's murderous assault except with the meaningless and prepackaged patter of television: "I'll be back with the answer in a minute" (312), "And this could represent the leading edge of some warmer air" (313). Mink becomes merely a channel for the complacent "chatter" or "idle talk" (to use Heidegger's terms) of television. The technology of the postmodern media merges with the technology of psycho-biology.

Throughout his work, DeLillo reveals that postmodernism marks a culmination rather than a break with the empiricist scientific tradition inaugurated in the seventeenth century. In so doing, DeLillo challenges a fundamental premise of contemporary postmodern thought: that postmodern thinking overcomes or "deconstructs" the false belief in absolute scientific objectivity. Like Heidegger, DeLillo suggests that the most basic assumption of postmodern thought – that man can know only that which he constructs –was already the explicit axiomatic basis of the modern scientific project. We would do well to remember that the reigning dogma of contemporary critical thought – that knowledge is the expression of power and that power constitutes knowledge – was the openly acknowledged starting point for those seventeenth-century thinkers such as Bacon, Descartes, and Hobbes who laid the philosophic foundation on which the modern scientific project was built.[17] Contemporary postmodern critics do not challenge the premises of scientific empiricism – they merely rediscover them when they declare that "man" can know only the world which he himself has made, the world which is an expression or representation of his arbitrary will or power.

5

> [Man] comes to the very brink of a precipitous fall; that is, he comes to the point where he himself will have to be taken as standing-reserve. Meanwhile man, precisely as the one so threatened, exalts himself to the posture of lord of the earth. In this way the impression comes to prevail that everything man encounters exists only insofar as it is his construct. This illusion gives rise in turn to one final delusion: It seems as though man everywhere and always encounters only himself. . . . *In truth, however, precisely nowhere does man today any longer encounter himself, i.e., his essence.*[18]

Heidegger is explicit in his condemnation of what we would now call postmodern existence, that state of affairs in which man has come to believe that everything he encounters is his own construct. For Heidegger as for DeLillo, the ironic consequence of his presumption is that man transforms himself into an object. What Heidegger calls the transformation of man into "standing-reserve" is more commonly recognized by contemporary critics as "reification." Having set out to reduce nature to an object and ultimately a construct, man succeeds in reducing human nature to an object or construct, a mere thing. The reification of contemporary man is a major theme in DeLillo's novels. In *Ratner's Star* a scientist named Cheops Feeley, backed by a vast multinational cartel interested in manipulating the international money curve, proposes to implant the "Leduc electrode" in the brain of DeLillo's protagonist, Billy Twillig. According to Feeley, Billy will become a paid consultant of the firm, a kind of biotechnical extension of the Space Brain computer that the cartel leases for its financial calculations. (The side effect of the surgical implant is that Billy, in true Cartesian fashion, would tend to reduce mentally all phenomena to their most basic elementary components. He would not be able to breathe without thinking of the sequence – heart, lungs, nostrils, oxygen, carbon dioxide, and so forth.) Feeley's proposed objectification of Billy is only a more literal version of what DeLillo sees as occurring on a vast cultural scale within postmodern America. The society which encourages the production of Dylar is one which tends to understand all human beings on the model of a thing. As Jack would have it, repeating the words of his son Heinrich, a contemporary pure product of postmodern culture, "We're the sum of our chemical impulses" (200).

Even in its most innocuous form, the objectification of contemporary man spreads through the culture via the everyday consumer activities of the American family. The relentless shopping of the Gladney family provides the chief means by which they constitute their existence. Especially when Jack and Babette suffer from an attack of anxiety and dread, they rush their family off to the supermarket for another quick fix of commodification:

> It seemed to me that Babette and I, in the mass and variety of our purchases, in the sheer plenitude those crowded bags suggested, the weight and size and number, the familiar package designs and vivid lettering, the giant sizes, the family bargain packs with Day-Glo sale stickers, in the sense of replenishment we felt, the sense of well-being, the security and contentment these products brought to some snug home in our souls – it seemed we had achieved a fullness of being that is not known to people who need less, expect less, who plan their lives around lonely walks in the evening. (20)

The supermarket is a powerful synecdoche for postmodern society. In it man encounters only that which he constructs or produces. So powerful is the illusion of omnipotence that he comes to understand himself as that which is constituted by those products. They provide his "fullness of being," a fullness of being counterposed to the seemingly alienated existence of those "who plan their lives around lonely walks in the evening." The metaphysical reversal to which Heidegger refers is complete. Authentic being, that knows itself to "ek-sist" or stick-out, is shunned in favor of *das Man*, the being that shops in herds.

Although the commodification of society may seem total and complete, the system of postmodern consumer culture is not entirely closed, nor is it truly comprehensive. Heidegger argues that, however dangerous and monolithic in appearance, the essence of technology may lead to a "turn" (*Kehre*). Quoting a favorite passage from Hölderlin's "Patmos," Heidegger suggests that technology might paradoxically offer a way beyond its own seemingly eternal thralldom:

> But where the danger is, grows
> The saving power also.

For the early Heidegger, *Dasein*'s existential orientation toward death facilitates the turn. Man's recognition of his personal finitude potentially frees him from the technological conceptualization of the world which divides everything into subject and object. It opens him up to other possible ways of understanding himself and his relationship to the world. *Angst*, or dread, which initially strikes man with such powerfully negative force, provides the potentially liberating experience par excellence. It is *Angst* that sets man on the way to a fundamental philosophic reassessment of the essence of technology, opens him up to the possibility that Being will reveal itself to him.

In one of his very few published interviews, DeLillo has suggested that the germinal idea for *White Noise* (one of the working titles of which was *The American Book of the Dead*) lay in the intimate connection between a kind of wonder or awe that we feel toward things and our deeply troubling anxiety over death:

> Our sense of fear – we avoid it because we feel it so deeply, so there is an intense conflict at work. I brought this conflict to the surface in the shape of Jack Gladney.
>
> I think it is something we all feel, something we almost never talk about, something that is *almost* there. I tried to relate it in *White Noise* to this other sense of transcendence that lies just beyond our touch. This extraordinary wonder of things is somehow related to

79

the extraordinary dread, to the death fear we try to keep beneath the surface of our perceptions.[19]

DeLillo's comments are in keeping with Heidegger's existential analysis, particularly as represented by *Being and Time*. Within this philosophic tradition, the acute perception of one's own mortality supplies the necessary preliminary step to an openness to Being, "the extraordinary wonder of things," that normally remains covered over by our refusal to confront personal finitude.

Although we have hitherto represented technology as the principal means by which man attempts to cover over his anxiety, and thereby evade his fear of death, for both Heidegger and DeLillo the very dangers of technology may ultimately prove a means of liberating man from the "essence of technology." In *White Noise*, one of the darkest jokes that the airborne toxic event plays on Jack Gladney is to threaten him with a death not particularly well defined, precise, or exact. After his exposure to Nyodene D., Jack holds the following conversation with a SIMUVAC employee:

> "Am I going to die?"
> "Not as such," he said.
> "What do you mean?"
> "Not in so many words."
> "How many words does it take?"
> "It's not a question of words. It's a question of years. We'll know more in fifteen years. In the meantime we definitely have a situation."
> "What will we know in fifteen years?"
> "If you're still alive at the time, we'll know that much more than we do now. Nyodene D. has a life span of thirty years. You'll have made it halfway through."
> "I thought it was forty years."
> "Forty years in the soil. Thirty years in the human body."
> "So, to outlive this substance, I will have to make it into my eighties. Then I can begin to relax." (140–1)

DeLillo's virtuoso dialogue is an absurdist drama in miniature. The threat of death is both real and utterly vague. It cannot be expressed in exact mathematical or linguistic terms. The technical analysis of the chemical agent and Jack's personal "history" reveals only that he will die; it does not tell him when he will die or what will bring about his death. The disturbingly funny conclusion that Jack draws – if he makes it into his eighties he can "begin to relax" – brilliantly illustrates his existential "situation." The fact is, Jack will die whether or not he has been exposed to Nyodene D. Obviously, if Jack lives into his eighties, he is closer to, not farther from, his own death. The airborne toxic event, though produced by a fully technological society, nevertheless replicates a primal and elementary human situation. It is, in words DeLillo borrows from Heidegger, a "flaw in the world picture" (229). Its manifest forms, a toxic cloud or "bracketed numbers with pulsing stars" on a computer screen (140) are mere representations, but nonetheless they are representations of an authentic existential threat. If the phenomenon of white noise serves as DeLillo's metaphor for the way in which technology covers over an existential perception of finitude (white noise is literally an artificially produced electronic noise invented to cover over the silence which disturbs workers in modern soundproof office buildings), it also functions as his trope for finitude itself, something just beyond "the range of human apprehension," below our daily level of consciousness, "sound all around," "uniform, white" (198). Technology, which promises (or threatens) to remove or cover over *Angst*, ultimately reproduces it in a new and vivid form.

6

Given the most recent controversy surrounding Heidegger's lengthy and intimate involvement with Nazism both before and after the famous turn in his philosophic thinking,[20] it is worthwhile for us to consider DeLillo's own particular interpretation of fascism in *White Noise* wherein he presents the cult of Hitler as the first postmodern political movement. As chairman of Hitler studies, Jack Gladney offers a course that focuses on the "continuing mass appeal of fascist tyranny, with special emphasis on parades, rallies and uniforms," but above all on "propaganda films" (25). As DeLillo sees it, fascism depends heavily upon modern technological means of representation, particularly film, for its success. For Jack, the special attraction of fascism lies in the apparent power of the carefully staged Nazi rally to ward off an existential confrontation with personal finitude: "Crowds came to form a shield against their own dying. To become a crowd is to keep out death. To break off from the crowd is to risk death as an individual, to face dying alone" (73). Hitler, or the image of Hitler (the two are the same in DeLillo), provide a particularly alluring shield against dying. As Murray, the émigré Jew from New York, succinctly puts it to Jack, "Some people are larger than life. Hitler is larger than death. You thought he would protect you. . . . On one level you wanted to conceal yourself in Hitler and his works. On another level you wanted to use him to grow in significance and strength" (287). Substitute the word "technology" for "Hitler" and the existential equation becomes clear. The two are interchangeable terms; both offer to conceal the isolated and anxiety-ridden individual from death, and both promise to increase the power and significance of that individual in order that he may conquer death.

Whether we understand fascism as an antimodern and antitechnological movement (as Heidegger sometimes did) or as a subspecies of technological postmodernism (as DeLillo does), we face considerable difficulty envisioning a political alternative to the technological world picture that would not open the way to fresh calamities on a global scale. The most basic political question remains unanswered: How does one move beyond a critique of the Enlightenment principles of the new science without reverting to bizarre forms of mystical and antihuman violence that characterize Jack Gladney in Germantown ("kill to live") or the murderous cult that gives DeLillo's novel *The Names* its title? To answer such a question, it would at the very least be necessary for us to reopen the question of how man should come to terms with human finitude. The existential critique of death reminds us that the modern technological project ultimately refuses to acknowledge any natural limitations on man, chief among which is human mortality. In so doing, the new science presumes to answer definitively the question of what man's relationship to nature ought to be. No less certain of itself, postmodernism, particularly when it understands itself as the antithesis rather than the culmination of the modern scientific project, confidently and unequivocally banishes from critical discussion the questions of human nature and of nature in general. Rather than entertain a careful and judicious debate over the possible meanings of such terms, postmodern criticism regards the questions themselves as illegitimate. Raising the grim specter of "universalist" discourse, postmodernism summarily declares "the end of philosophy." But it may well be that a reconsideration of these fundamental questions would not necessarily culminate in the universalist dogmas that their detractors fear. The reexploration of basic if neglected philosophic questions might provide the firmest foundation yet for a critique of such dogmas and of the dreaded social consequences alleged to follow from them.

In any case, if we are to reopen these questions, we must recognize that it is both impractical and imprudent to insist that each and every individual in a political community become "resolute" toward death (to employ a Heideggerian phrase) or remain continuously at the ready, poised and open for Being to reveal itself. Moreover, we should openly acknowledge that technology and its essence have much too powerful a hold on contemporary society for us to expect them to relinquish their grasp peacefully. Paradoxically, by recognizing the practical dangers inherent in any transformation of society along lines suggested by the critique of technology, we might begin to challenge one of the underlying assumptions that originally gave rise to the modern scientific project, and that has subtly shaped the context of all debate concerning the essence of technology since its inception. The Enlightenment, broadly conceived, raised the stakes of its theoretical enterprise by claiming that it was possible for human society as a whole to become fully rational and self-conscious. What was previously thought to be of potential interest to only a few rather odd or unusual individuals the Enlightenment promised to make the common inheritance of the entire human community. However tempting this utopian vision might be, it is possible that with each new attempt to transform all men into philosophers the Enlightenment tends only to encourage more and more extreme forms of unenlightened reaction, resistance, and revolution.

One of the great merits of DeLillo's fiction is the degree to which it remains deeply suspicious of the political prudence of all outspoken and "practicing" theoreticians. In *White Noise*, as in *Ratner's Star* and *The Names*, DeLillo suggests that attempts to impose conceptual clarity and theoretical rigor on the habits of many human beings all too often tend to result in novel and sometimes dangerous forms of mystification. "In theory," as Murray says, "violence is a form of rebirth" (290). Consequently one has to "kill to live" (291). *In theory.* The problem with theoreticians like Murray is their willingness to recommend theoretical solutions with unpredictable but all too palpable consequences, such as those visited on the likes of Willie Mink (himself a rather Faustian figure whose theories bear terribly on Babette). DeLillo's antitheoretical prudence finds expression in the comments of a nun who tends Jack's wounds in Germantown: "It is our task in the world to believe things no one else takes seriously. To abandon such beliefs completely, the human race would die" (318). DeLillo does not suggest that the sister's faith is grounded in metaphysical truth; as a self-confessed anachronism, she implicitly acknowledges that her belief is in some profound sense a performance for the benefit of others. Her prudence suggests that the community as a whole cannot live with the truth, so better to offer comforting fictions that allow the majority of citizens to live in a state of relative harmony and benign mystification. However challenging and disturbing his anarchistic writing may be for the perceptive reader, DeLillo's reluctance to become identified with any specific political agenda, his refusal to offer a wholesale plan for social transformation, his steady insistence that he does not "have a program," should be understood as the prudence of a theoretically sophisticated novelist who recognizes the terrible dangers that theory may pose when it offers to become practice.[21]

NOTES

1. For example, see Stuart Johnson's "Extraphilosophical Instigations in Don DeLillo's *Running Dog,*" *Contemporary Literature* 26 (1985): 80. Also compare *Great Jones Street* (New York: Vintage, 1973), p. 61, with Heidegger's *Being and Time,* trans. John Macquarrie and Edward Robinson (New York: Harper & Row, 1962), pp. 102–7.

2. See, for example, Frank Lentricchia, "*Libra* as Postmodern Critique," *South Atlantic Quarterly* 89 (1990): 433–5, and John Frow, "The Last Things Before the Last: Notes on *White Noise,*" ibid., pp. 413–30.

3. Martin Heidegger, "The Question Concerning Technology," in *The Question Concerning Technology and Other Essays,* trans. William Lovitt (New York: Harper & Row, 1977), p. 16.

4. DeLillo has been relatively circumspect about his political sympathies. He has nevertheless made it quite clear that his criticisms of a consumer culture notwithstanding, his political opinions are not those of a Marxist like Lee Harvey Oswald: "I don't have a political theory or doctrine I'm espousing. . . . Certainly the left-wing theories of Oswald do not coincide with my own. I don't have a program." See Anthony DeCurtis, "'An Outsider in This Society': An Interview with Don DeLillo," *South Atlantic Quarterly* 89 (1990): 303.

5. Don DeLillo, *Ratner's Star* (New York: Vintage, 1976), p. 236.

6. Consider, for example, Heidegger's comments on Descartes in "The Age of the World Picture" (*The Question Concerning Technology,* pp. 127, 139–40), as well as *What Is a Thing?,* trans. W. B. Barton, Jr., and Vera Deutsch (South Bend, Ind.: Gateway, 1967), pp. 78, 98–106, and *Being and Time,* pp. 89–101.

7. See Charles Molesworth, "Don DeLillo's *Perfect Starry Night,"* *South Atlantic Quarterly* 89 (1990): 383.

8. See Frank Lentricchia, "*Libra* as Postmodern Critique," pp. 431–3.

9. Niccolò Machiavelli, *Discourses on the First Ten Books of Titus Livy,* trans. Leslie J. Walker (Harmondsworth, U.K.: Penguin, 1970), p. 97.

10. Heidegger, "The Question Concerning Technology," p. 28.

11. See Max Horkheimer and Theodor Adorno, *Dialectic of Enlightenment,* trans. John Cumming (New York: Continuum, 1972), pp. xi–xvii, 3–42.

12. On this paradoxical quality of the media, see Heidegger, "The Thing," in *Poetry, Language, Thought,* trans. Albert Hofstadter (New York: Harper, 1971), pp. 165–6.

13. For a similar analysis, see Eugene Goodheart, "Don DeLillo and the Cinematic Real," *South Atlantic Quarterly* 89 (1990): 361–3.

14. See Martin Heidegger, *Being and Time,* pp. 279–311.

15. See especially Heidegger, *Being and Time,* pp. 383–423.

16. For DeLillo the child is the liminal case. Babette's child Wilder cannot yet speak and has not yet come to fear death, hence his miraculous ride across the heavily trafficked highway. The urgency with which Babette and Jack cling to Wilder and seek solace from his presence is connected to their longing for a similarly unselfconscious state (289). Unlike the animal, however, the child possesses linguistic ability and the fear of death *in potentia.* For an older premodern philosophic

tradition, this distinction is a *natural* one. It is philosophically significant that logos and self-consciousness (in the form of recognition of one's own finitude) are connected.

17. See Heidegger, "The Age of the World Picture," pp. 127, 142; Leo Strauss, *Natural Right and History* (Chicago: University of Chicago Press, 1950), p. 173; and Horkheimer and Adorno, *Dialectic of Enlightenment*, pp. 3–5.
18. Heidegger, "The Question Concerning Technology," p. 27.
19. Anthony DeCurtis, "Interview with Don DeLillo," p. 301. DeLillo has said of *White Noise*, "It's about death on the individual level." See Sharon K. Hall, ed., *Contemporary Literary Criticism* (Detroit: Gale Research, 1985), 39:115.
20. See Luc Ferry and Alain Renaut, *Heidegger and Modernity*, trans. Franklin Phillip (Chicago: University of Chicago Press, 1990), pp. 55–80.
21. See Anthony DeCurtis, "An Interview with Don DeLillo," p. 303.

5

Tales of the Electronic Tribe

FRANK LENTRICCHIA

The first 11 days of the Persian Gulf war have had the feeling of a surreal spectator sport here, with the President constantly flicking television channels in the study off the Oval Office and with other senior officials gathered in semicircles with sandwiches around the television set. . . . Robert M. Gates, the deputy national security advisor, has found the obsessive television watching at the White House so distracting – and perhaps diminishing to the myth of privileged information – that he refuses to even turn on his office television set now, loyally waiting for reports from the Situation Room.

But even that top-secret intelligence, widely presumed to be fuller and more accurate, has been infected by the television coverage.

"The problem is that it's hard to sort out the information because the CNN stuff has a way of trickling into the intelligence," another Bush advisor said, referring to Cable News Network, the potent new entry in Washington's alphabet soup. "We get the intelligence reports and they include stuff that's on CNN. Then we get another report that seems to confirm what the first report said, but it turns out that they're just using a later CNN broadcast. CNN confirming CNN."

–*New York Times*, January 29, 1991

"**POSTMODERNISM**": Our key term of cultural self-consciousness – a word we utter from within the dark wood in order to define not merely contemporary art and literature of the first world, but also who we are, how we live. One of the characters in Don DeLillo's first novel, *Americana* (1971) – in witty anticipation of the current controversy over the idea of the postmodern – says that television came over on the *Mayflower*. If television is the quintessential technological constituent of the postmodern temper (so it goes), and postmodernism the ethos of the electronic society, then with twenty years of hindsight on De-Lillo's book we can say that what actually came over on the *Mayflower* was postmodernism itself, the founding piece of Ameri-

87

cana. "America": imagined rather than geographic space, the very form of postmodern desire.

In that first novel DeLillo defines American desire as nothing other than desire for the universal third person – the "he" or "she" we dream about from our armchairs in front of the TV, under the strong stimulus of Madison Avenue, originally dreamt by the first immigrants, the Pilgrims on their way over, the object of the dream being the person those Pilgrims would become: a new self because a New World. Sitting in front of TV is like a perpetual Atlantic crossing – the desire for and the discovery of America constantly reenacted in our move from first-person consciousness to third: from the self we are, but would leave behind, to the self we would become. Advertising may have discovered and exploited the economic value of the person we all want to be, but the pilgrim-consumer dreaming on the *Mayflower,* or on the *New Mayflower* in front of television, invented that person.

The distinction between the real and the fictional can't be sustained – not on the *Mayflower,* not while watching TV, nowhere in America, certainly not in the burgeoning variety of theories of postmodernism. The undesirability of the distinction between the real and the fictional is the key meaning, even, of being an American. To be real in America is to be in the position of the "I" who must negate I, leave I behind in a real or metaphoric Europe. So in order for America to be America the original moment of yearning for the third-person must be ceaselessly renewed. One of the harsher charges of postmodern theorists (especially of the French type) is that America has perfected the practice of cultural imperialism; everyone in the world now – Islamic cultures perhaps excepted – wants to be an American. As I follow the implications of DeLillo's mythic history of television, that's exactly what the world's always wanted, long before there was a political entity called America to be scapegoated for the phenomenon of American desire.

In the third chapter of *White Noise* there is a brief scene that extends this surprising history of television. "THE MOST PHOTOGRAPHED BARN IN AMERICA" is the ostensible subject of the scene; the real subject is the electronic medium of the image as the active context of contemporary existence in America. TV, a productive medium of the image, is only one (albeit dominant) technological expression of an entire environment of the image. But unlike TV, which is an element in the contemporary landscape, the environment of the image *is* the landscape – it is what (for us) "landscape" has become, and it can't be switched off with the flick of a wrist. For this environment-as-electronic-medium radically constitutes contemporary consciousness and therefore (such as it is) contemporary community – it guarantees that we are a people of, by, and for the image. Measured against TV advertising's manipulation of the image of the third person, the economic goals of which are pretty clear, and clearly susceptible to class analysis from the left – it is obvious who the big beneficiaries of such manipulations are – the environment of the image in question in *White Noise* appears far less concretely in focus. Less apprehensible, less empirically encounterable – therefore more insidious in its effects.

The first-person narrator of *White Noise*, Jack Gladney, a college professor, drives to the tourist attraction known as the most photographed barn in America, and he takes with him his new colleague, Murray Jay Siskind, a professor of popular culture, a smart émigré from New York City to middle America. The tourist attraction is pastorally set, some twenty miles from the small city where the two reside and teach, and all along the way there are natural things to be taken in, presumably, though all the nature that is experienced (hardly the word, but it will have to do) is noted in a flat, undetailed, and apparently unemotional declarative: "There were meadows and apple orchards." And the traditional picturesque of rural life is similarly registered: "White fences trailed through the rolling fields." The strategically unenergized prose of these traditional moments is an index to the passing of both a literary convention and an older America. The narrator continues in his recessed way while his companion comments (lectures, really) on the tourist site, which is previewed for them (literally) by several signs, spaced every few miles along the way, announcing the attraction in big block letters. There is a booth where a man sells postcards and slides of the barn; there is an elevated spot from which the crowd of tourists snap their photos.

Gladney's phlegmatic narrative style in this passage is thrown into high relief by the ebullience of his friend's commentary. Murray does all the talking, like some guru drawing his neophyte into a new world which the neophyte experiences in a shocked state of half-consciousness situated somewhere between the older world where there were objects of perception like barns and apple orchards and the strange new world where the object of perception is perception itself: a packaged perception, a "sight" (in the genius of the vernacular), not a "thing." What they view is the view of a thing. What Murray reveals is that "no one sees the barn" because once "you've seen the signs about the barn, it becomes impossible to see the barn." This news about the loss of the referent, the dissolving of the object into its representations (the road signs, the photos), is delivered not with nostalgia for a lost world of the real but with joy: "We're not here to capture an image, we're here to maintain one. Every photograph reinforces the aura."

In between Murray's remarks, Jack Gladney reports on the long silences and the background noise – a new kind of choral commentary, "the incessant clicking of shutter release buttons, the rustling of crank levers that advanced the film" – and on the tourists ritually gathered in order to partake, as Murray says, of "a kind of spiritual surrender." So not only can't we get outside the aura, we really don't want to. We prefer not to know what the barn was like before it was photographed because its aura, its technological glow, its soul, is our production, it is us. "We're part of the aura," says Murray, and knowing we're a part is tantamount to the achievement of a new identity – a collective selfhood brought to birth in the moment of contact with an "accumulation of nameless energies," in the medium of representation synonymous with the conferring of fame, charisma, desirable selfhood. "We're here, we're now," says Murray, as if he were affirming the psychic wholeness of the community. "The thousands who were here in the past, those who will come here in the future. We've agreed to be part of a collective perception."

What will trip up any reader intent on extrapolating DeLillo's views on postmodernism – as if the passage on the most photographed barn were a miniature essay, and a transparent one at that – is the doubly distanced relationship of writer to his materials. If we remember that Murray – a character, after all – does most of the talking, that his talking is filtered through a character of special narrative authority – a first-person narrator – then the question becomes not what does DeLillo think of Murray's ideas but what does Gladney think of them, and only then might we ask how does DeLillo position his thoughts of Gladney's thoughts of Murray. The regress is not infinite, but it is pretty thick and has the effect of throwing readers back on their own resources of judgment without the comfort of firm authorial guidance.

It's hard to miss the excitement of Murray's dialogue, the rhythmic blooding of his ideas:

> "What was the barn like before it was photographed? . . . What did it look like, how was it different from other barns, how was it similar to other barns? We can't answer these questions because we've read the signs, seen the people snapping the pictures. We can't get outside the aura. We're part of the aura. We're here, we're now."

Hard to call that ironic talk (though elsewhere Murray will show himself to be the devil's own ironist). No satiric voice utters the phrases "spiritual surrender," "collective perception," or "religious experience." Have we somehow come back to the world, beyond the alienation that a number of writers made synonymous with the literature of modernism? The community despaired of by nostalgic modernists located, at last, not in some premodern village of artisans, or some fascist state, but in postmodern society, godless and bereft of tradition though it is? Community sprung wholly from the technology of the image? Can this be serious? What does Gladney think? At the end of Murray's outburst Jack says: "He seemed immensely pleased by this." In light of his caustic treatment of contemporary culture everywhere else in the book, this is a curiously withheld remark, as if he can't quite get a fix on Murray.

The more typical Murray is a subversive whose humor depends on our recognition that postmodern values are the dominant ones of our culture. When Jack tells him that there is something perplexing about someone they know, Murray solves the puzzle with "He's flesh-colored." The typical Jack is the same sort of humorist who enjoys tripping on the postmodern. He asks a worker for a state agency called SIMUVAC (short for "simulated evacuation"),

"Are you people sure you're ready for a simulation? You may want to wait for one more massive spill. Get your timing down." People who speak of using the real as a model deserve sardonic treatment. But in the scene of the most photographed barn the typically witty Murray and Jack are strangely absent. Is community a specially honored value of Gladney's, exactly what his irony may not touch? One worth cherishing, wherever it is found? Does the passage on the most photographed barn represent a new literary form comfortably based on the technology of electronics? And shall we now speak of the postmodern idyll?

Walter Benjamin once cited Proust on the phenomenology of the aura as the experience which gives access to tradition: "monuments and pictures" of the past presenting themselves "only beneath the delicate veil which centuries of love and reverence on the part of so many admirers have woven about them." To experience monuments and pictures in this way is to experience intimacy with those who have cared about art history; it is to experience the entry into community, aesthetically mediated over time, as a variegated tapestry of loving response. And it is precisely such experience of community that Benjamin would deny our age of mechanical reproduction, the age decisively marked by the advent of photography, which is (Benjamin again) the advent of the decline of aura, the loss of tradition and the historical sense.

But Benjamin's deadly camera which returns no human gaze may be the mediator of a new kind of community, wherein all distinctive selfhood is extinguished in a new art form whose mass cultural presence glows at postmodernism's holy place, the site of the most photographed barn. DeLillo's point, unlike Benjamin's, is not the nostalgic one that aura is in decline, but that its source has been replaced. The question he poses in all but words is, What strange new form of human collectivity is born in the postmodern moment of aura, and at what price?

It probably can't be said too strongly: *White Noise* is a first-person narrative – a fact of literary structure that will turn out to be decisive for all that can be said about the book's take on contemporary America and the issues that cluster about the cloudy concept of postmodernism. Like Melville's Ishmael, Twain's Huck, and

Fitzgerald's Nick Carraway, DeLillo's Jack Gladney is a sharp observer and commentator who at the same time participates – often to the reader's bewilderment – in an action which fatally shapes him, so that he will not understand with total lucidity what it is he observes, or who he himself really is, or the extent to which he, Jack Gladney, is the less than self-possessed voice of a culture that he would subject to criticism and satire. The major consequence of the book's materials being filtered through a character named Gladney rather than directly through a writer named DeLillo is a complexity beyond the narrator's ken: a terrible complicity in the horrors narrated that may be the real point of the writer's (not Gladney's) discomforting perspective.

Like a number of novels in the mainstream of American literature, *White Noise* appears to be motivated by a double purpose: to write social criticism of its author's place and time, while showing its readers the difficulty of doing so with a clean conscience and an un-self-deluded mind. This sort of doubly motivated writing, from Melville to DeLillo, gives no comfort because while it trades upon the desire to fix what seems most dreadful in our culture it insists on showing us that what especially needs fixing is the intelligent and sensitive fixers themselves. *Moby Dick, Huckleberry Finn, The Great Gatsby,* and *White Noise* are exemplary first person narratives in the American grain for the reason that their critical authority cannot be abstracted from their trapped and partially subverted first-person tellers; abstracted and then assigned to a kingly sort of storyteller – an omniscient narrator who gives the illusion of being uncontaminated by the issues he would excoriate and who would therefore perform the role of good cultural doctor, safely inoculated from the diseases that plague the rest of us. The reader of *White Noise* may be bewildered, but such bewilderment is the strategic effect of DeLillo's most important formal decision.

Point of view in narrative produces its most immediate effects (especially in the first-person mode) sentence by sentence where it is embodied sensuously in the sound of the storyteller's voice. DeLillo gives us his Jack Gladney in full tonal profile in the brief five-paragraph first chapter of the novel, which begins with a cutting description of an annual autumn ritual at what are called the finer American colleges and universities – the lavish return of students and admiring parents – and ends on a note of poignancy beyond the reach of the narrator's usual irony: "On telephone poles all over town there are homemade signs concerning lost dogs and cats, sometimes in the handwriting of a child." The opening and closing sentences of a number of this novel's chapters are so unusually weighted with emotive freight that they seem discontinuous and self-sufficient, virtually leaving the text, so much the better to haunt the mind. The last sentence of the first chapter works that way, surprising us as an expression of sheer domestic sentiment unpredictable in context – intriguing precisely because it appears to be ungrounded in the knowing and well-weathered voice that begins the chapter; the voice that takes wicked pleasure in making lists of the bounty that students unload when they return to classes:

> the stereo sets, radios, personal computers; small refrigerators and table ranges; the cartons of phonograph records and cassettes; the hairdryers and styling irons; the tennis rackets, soccer balls, hockey and lacrosse sticks, bows and arrows; the controlled substances, the birth control pills and devices; the junk food still in shopping bags – onion-and-garlic chips, nacho thins, peanut creme patties, Waffelos and Kabooms, fruit chews and toffee popcorn; the Dum-Dum pops, the Mistic mints.

This narrator can read the signs of social class in the commodities we command, and he enjoys passing judgment dryly, in the proportions and arrangements that he gives to the items of his list: more items of junk food than anything else, and those, by providing closure to both list and first paragraph, perform a retrospective, if implicit, evaluation of the whole. Those who can possess such things – sports-mad, narcissistic, pleasure-seeking – are the pure American products of a culture addicted to junk food, the representations of a junky, because a mass, culture, the human Dum-Dum pops. This narrator (he describes himself as a "witness" to this "spectacle" of return: and he says "spectacle" as if what he sees were one of the primary staged entertainments of his culture), this narrator is tired. He's seen it too many times, for twenty-one years to be exact. Nevertheless his weariness is disturbing because it is rooted in the banality of everyday life, weariness apparently unavoidable. The key cultural marker in his list (the first of many he will give us) is the innocent little definite article: He says the stereo sets, the hairdryers, and the junk food ("The station wagons arrived at noon" is the way the book begins) because he's evoking generic objects and events, things seen everywhere and all the time – relentlessly repetitious experience being something like the point of mass culture in an advanced capitalist economy. With perception so grooved on the routine, the affective consequence follows rigorously. Gladney's ironies bespeak boredom, an enervation of spirit, and, beneath it all, an intimation of a Hell whose origin lies in the high modernist fear that the life of consciousness, especially its aesthetic possibilities, will become like the mass culture that modernists mainly loathe, often parody, and sometimes even love.

The implicit indictment in Gladney's list of predictable first world wonders is leveled not at all the rich kids and their parents – the power of money inequitably distributed – but at the options of the economically privileged, the triviality of this culture's gifts. Where are the books? Shoved, in Gladney's list, ignominiously between boots, stationery, sheets, pillows, and quilts. Whatever their titles (no doubt best not to know them) these books are things like other things, commodities, too, or – in the most question-begging of all economic terms – *goods*, but not good enough to deserve verbal differentiation (we know them only as "books"), unlike the English and Western saddles, the Waffelos and Kabooms. And what could a book really signify in a series whose rolling rhythms make it hard to tell the difference between an English saddle and a Kaboom? There are many things to be said about living in the United States in the late twentieth century, and Gladney's list, whose deepest subject is cultural democracy, is one of them.

And the torpid Gladney can get no satisfaction when he turns his gaze upon this autumn spectacle's human figures, who find the solidarity of their community in displays of style and stylistic mimicry (in a postmodern culture, a hard thing to distinguish), in striking the easily readable pose, in trading upon their culture's most stable currency, that of the image:

> The students greet each other with comic cries and gestures of sodden collapse. Their summer has been bloated with criminal pleasures, as always. The parents stand sun-dazed near their automobiles, seeing images of themselves in every direction. The conscientious suntans. The well-made faces and wry looks. They feel a sense of renewal, of communal recognition. The women crisp and alert, in diet trim, knowing people's names . . . something about [their husbands] suggesting massive insurance coverage. This assembly of station wagons, as much as anything they might do in the course of the year, more than formal liturgies or laws, tells the parents they are a collection of the like-minded and the spiritually akin, a people, a nation.

In the mocking crescendo of his final phrases, Gladney's voice builds to the corrosive authority of satire. Here is image and style classically, suspiciously viewed as tricky, seductive surface, style and image as absence of substantial selfhood, the void at the core. The students have watched too many bad actors; the remark about "massive insurance coverage" is funny and totally nasty.

Having seen enough of the spectacle of return, Gladney leaves the panoramic perch of his office and walks home, noting along the way more numbing simulcra (the "Greek revival and Gothic churches"). Then suddenly there is a shift in focus and we feel ourselves for a moment on the familiar terrain of the realist novel. He tells us he lives at the end of a quiet street "in what was once a wooded area with deep ravines." This turn from critical to novelistic observation is enhanced with a moody reverie on the past pressing into the present; he mentions that now, just beyond his backyard, there is an expressway, and at night, as he and his wife settle into sleep, they hear the "remote and steady murmur" of traffic moving past: haunted, foggy sounds, as if the cars, moving over the place of the old wooded area, were moving over a graveyard, as if they were giving voice to something strange, "as of dead souls babbling at the edge of dream."

Before we can measure the effect of this tonal shift – it seems a lament over modernization – the tone quickly shifts again and the narrator tells us flatly who he is: chairman of the department of Hitler studies at the College-on-the-Hill (the "College-on-the-Hill," we know where it is, we know it well), who invented Hitler studies in America in March of 1968. This piece of information is followed by the first chapter's oddest sentence: "It was a cold bright day with intermittent winds out of the east." Straight or deadpan? A joke about the way we talk these days about the weather, with our voices indentured to the jargon of what is called meteorology? A joke that stings us for our inability to muster "real" voice, "real" speech, even about – or is it especially about? – matters so ordinary? Or is the sentence delivered unawares, just the way Jack talks sometimes, like a weatherman? Self-parody or a weird, because unconscious, form of "pastiche," a term whose very meaning assumes an act of deliberation? After inquiring in Jack's sort of voice whether the parents were costumed in cable-knit sweaters and hacking jackets, Babette, Jack's wife, makes the point: "Not that we don't have a station wagon ourselves."

Our strolling narrator notes another ritual act: "At Fourth and Elm" (we know those streets) "the cars turn left for the super-market," as if they never turn right, perhaps because the super-market is another of this novel's communal sites – and that is why they always turn left. And now the final sentence about the home-made signs concerning lost dogs and cats, in the handwriting of innocence itself, to which Jack, who would seem the innocent's very antithesis, is nevertheless drawn. The Jack who comes to us bearing the satirist's gift of criticism to his culture comes bearing pathos and portents as well. That sentence about the "spiritually akin, a people, a nation" seemed purely caustic, but perhaps it was only partially so. But what could "partially caustic" mean, and how we do define a point of view that can accommodate that sort of tone?

In the usual sense of what it means to say that a novel has plot, *White Noise* has no plot. But plotlessness is itself a controlled effect of this book because until its concluding chapters (when Gladney decides that he will put some plot into his life) the novel is nar-rated by a man who fears plots in both conspiratorial and literary senses – a distinction hard to make in DeLillo's world – and who therefore resists them, even prays for plotlessness, a life un-governed by design and intention: "Let's enjoy these aimless days while we can, I told myself, fearing some kind of deft accelera-tion." That's the surprising first sentence of the fifth chapter through which DeLillo manages to let Jack speak his wish and fear at the same time. The apparently unprepared appearance of the sentence is a sign of the undriven, episodic character of the first third of the book in particular, and its portentous and out-of-the-blue quality is an indication that his narrator is working hard to repress an obscurely grounded anxiety that something horrible is about to happen to him and his family. There really is a story at work in Gladney's life, one he'd prefer not to know about because it's a story over which he exerts no authorial control, a story, nevertheless, he will be caught up in as he tells it from the edges of his consciousness, half-ignorant of what it is he narrates.

"Waves and Radiation," the title of the first of the book's three sections, is composed of twenty brief chapters, most of which seem disconnected from one another. In *White Noise* disconnection is the narrative mark of a mind taking pleasure in its meandering progression, a mind that avoids causal coherence by skipping from topic to topic: his wife, the children – his and hers – who live with them, his students, his colleagues (especially those in popular culture), the supermarket, the shopping mall, television, his ex-wife, the kids who don't live with them, what it's like to live in a small town called Blacksmith. (Murray says, "I can't help being happy in a town called Blacksmith.")

The major effect of "Waves and Radiation" is of leisurely description interrupted every so often by the question that obsesses Jack and Babette – "Who will die first?" – and by those startling sentences that open and close a number of the chapters. Like the one about a man in a rocker on his front porch, glimpsed in passing, who "stares into space"; or the one about Jack's oldest son, only in his early teens, already with a hairline in dramatic retreat; or the one about Jack waking "in the grip of a death sweat"; or the one about the day the youngest child cried for almost seven straight hours, for no reason that anyone, including a doctor, can discern; or the most telling one of all, which opens the ninth chapter: "They had to evacuate the grade school on Tuesday." Such moments in the novel function as terrorized punctuation, a sort of tip of the withheld subjective life of Jack Gladney, teasing signs of something outside his voice, rarely seen, an index to a level in his dense, meticulous, and disquietingly observed description to which Jack can give no overt interpretation because he seems not conscious of how the intensely observed items in his notation all come together to form the motive of his terror, his unwitting theme. "Theme": exactly what you can't observe but must interpret, a barely audible refrain that will clue us in to the function of "Waves and Radiation" – the establishment of the novel's true setting. Not Blacksmith, middle America, but the environment unintentionally produced by advanced technology, the effects of technology, the by-products, the fallout.

The pervasive tension that gives the reader perspective and constant access to the novel's atmosphere of pathos – what DeLillo knows and Jack does not want to know but half-knows – is that character is a function of setting. In *White Noise*, DeLillo rewrites the classic naturalist novel. Unlike, say, Dreiser's Carrie, Jack is endowed with intellectual power, yet in the end he is no less a plaything of his "American environments" (as the popular culture program at Jack's college is called). Jack is a strong reader, a ceaseless professor, but DeLillo opens a space between him and the novel's setting across which Jack's interpretive energy cannot jump. The tension between what DeLillo knows but cannot say directly, and what Jack knows, stimulates the reader to make sense of the novel's setting by connecting widely separated facts of description: Jack notes "our brightly colored food"; he notes the stack of "three-hour colored flame sawdust and wax logs" on his front porch; the fruit bins in the supermarket where "Everything seemed to be in season, sprayed, burnished, bright." Having grasped that embedded series, maybe the reader will draw a connection between it and Jack's brooding question about Heinrich's hairline: "Have I raised him, unwittingly, in the vicinity of a chemical dump site, in the path of air currents that carry industrial wastes capable of producing scalp degeneration, glorious sunsets? (People say the sunsets around here were not nearly so stunning thirty or forty years ago.)" When we eat "our brightly colored food," what else – unwittingly – do we eat? What do the Gladneys inhale for the pleasure of watching the colored flame of their sawdust and wax logs? Is it important that Jack and Babette know exactly why two of their closet doors open by themselves? Jack hears with paranoid apprehension the quiet rumble of the clothes

dryer, the radiator, the refrigerator, the thermostat buzzing for unknown reasons. Do these standard friends of the standard American family give off something other than harmless sound? Just
how far does our unwittingness extend? Hazardous waste dumps
are bad, but at least we know where they are. Electromagnetic
radiation (Heinrich will drive this point home) is the menace outside sensory apprehension. "Where do you think all the deformed
babies are coming from?" Heinrich asks. "Radio and TV, that's
where."

"Waves and Radiation" is all about the white noise, actual and
metaphoric, that constitutes the setting of a postmodern life, an
environment more or less in focus – less rather than more because
not a direct object of perception like traditional novelistic and
premodern environments, the city and the country. And the less in
focus the environment, the more our paranoia is enhanced, not
clinically but as a general (and reasonable) psychic condition of
privileged first world citizens. But there is a type of white noise –
more cultural than technological, another difficult distinction in
postmodern context – *more* rather than less in focus, more in focus
especially if you're a Jack or a Murray, a type of the intellectual
found flourishing (but hardly exclusively so) in the humanities
wing of institutions of higher learning: the habitually ironic cultural critic, the urban intellectual guerrilla finely attuned to the presence of the media as powerful shaper of the way we crystallize
ourselves for ourselves and for others; who believes in his own
freedom just because he knows how the culture industry works;
who believes in the West's classic philosophic dictum, that self-
knowledge sets us free, though he's generally too cool to say he
believes in anything.

When Murray tells us that he "can't help being happy in a town
called Blacksmith," he is telling us how happy he is to note, for the
delectation of anyone who might be listening, the gap between
word and thing, the nostalgia of the name. When Jack asks Murray where he's living, Murray responds:

> "In a rooming house. . . . Seven or eight boarders. . . . A woman
> who harbors a terrible secret. A man with a haunted look. A man
> who never comes out of his room. A woman who stands by the
> mailbox for hours, waiting for something that never seems to arrive.

A man with no past. A woman with a past. There is a smell about
the place of unhappy lives in the movies that I really respond to."
"Which one are you?" I said.
"I'm the Jew. What else would I be?"

Murray knows all about the movies, how they shape the texture of
what he sees, and he knows how to turn his knowledge into
playfulness. But Jack's immediate reflection implies that there is
impotence beneath Murray's postmodern ironies, that what comes
before the image – though itself maybe movie-generated – is
nevertheless painfully real, a sadness and deprivation that motivates the story of Murray's search for the third person of his
dreams:

> There was something touching about the fact that Murray was
> dressed almost totally in corduroy. I had the feeling that since the
> age of eleven in his crowded plot of concrete he'd associated this
> sturdy fabric with higher learning in some impossibly distant and
> tree-shaded place. . . . The small stiff beard, confined to his chin
> and unaccompanied by a mustache, seemed an optional compo-
> nent, to be stuck on or removed as circumstances warranted.

Is Jack master of himself, this postmodern Longfellow with a
Chaplinesque eye for cultural anatomy, who delivers the maxims
by which we frighten ourselves?

> When times are bad, people feel compelled to overeat. Blacksmith is
> full of obese adults and children, baggy-pantsed, short-legged, wad-
> dling. They struggle to emerge from compact cars; they don sweat-
> shirts and run in families across the landscape; they walk down the
> street with food in their faces; they eat in stores, cars, parking lots,
> on bus lines and movie lines, under the stately trees.

The contemplative distance of that meditation and the superiority
it implies are deliciously subverted about two hundred pages later
when the Gladneys engage in a feeding frenzy in a fast-food park-
ing lot, after times have indeed turned bad for them. But we don't
have to wait that long for Jack's culture to exact its revenge. The
scene is the bedroom of the adult Gladneys; Babette is about to
perform an act that Jack hugely enjoys. She will read to him from
their historically wide-ranging collection of pornographic literature. Jack chooses; Babette reads:

101

"But I don't want you to choose anything that has men inside women, quote-quote, or men entering women. 'I entered her.' 'He entered me.' We're not lobbies or elevators. . . . Can we agree on that? . . ."

"Agreed."

"'I entered here and began to thrust.'"

"I'm in total agreement," I said.

"'Enter me, enter me, yes, yes.'"

"Silly usage, absolutely."

"'Insert yourself, Rex. I want you inside me, entering hard, entering deep. Yes, now, oh.'"

The funniest moment in the passage occurs not in dialogue, however, but in Jack's immediate interior reflection. "I began to feel an erection stirring," he says. "How stupid and out of context" – that his last hold on nature should be the effect of a quotation. Jack, a parodist of contemporary jargons, and, like Murray, a cultural ecologist, knows better. That is why he says "stupid." But knowledge and wit cannot undo his victimage by the cultural ecosystem: the "eco" of ecology, from the Greek *oikos*, means "house." No "out of context" because no getting outside our cultural house.

Just how far down and in media culture has penetrated is illustrated by the novel's formally most astonishing moment – an effort to represent the irruption of the unconscious – variations on which are played throughout. A deep refrain – like a line of poetic chant, with strong metrical structure – is placed by itself in privileged typographical space, part of no paragraph or dialogue, without quotes and related to nothing that comes before or after: a break in the text never reflected upon because Jack never hears it. It is, of course, Jack who speaks the line because *White Noise* is a first-person novel, and it could therefore be no one else. Jack in these moments is possessed, a mere medium who speaks:

Dacron, Orlon, Lycra Spandex
MasterCard, Visa, American Express
Leaded, Unleaded, Superunleaded

Jacques Lacan said the unconscious is structured like a language. He forgot to add the words "of Madison Avenue."

From the cultural and technological density of the first section of *White Noise* two actions emerge and eventually come together in the near fatal act that shapes the novel's concluding chapters. One of those actions is Jack's effort to learn the significance of an experimental and illegally obtained medication secretly ingested by Babette and known to him only as "Dylar." Not known to him until far into the novel's final section (entitled "Dylarama") is that Dylar is Babette's desperate response to the question "Who will die first?" Madison Avenue captures the unconscious; industrial pollution enhances the beauty of nature (what Jack calls "postmodern" sunsets); Dylar, ultimate postmodern drug, would inhibit fear of death, nature's final revenge on postmodern culture. What we see from a Dylaramic prospect is everyday life in America as a 360-degree display of what are called "controlled substances," America as the culture of the Dylar effect.

The other action that emerges quite literally from the novel's setting is the matter of deep plot, the process that motivates the novel's agents. In the classic naturalist vision of *White Noise,* it is the novel's setting that "acts," the novel's setting that drives the novel's human agents, and by so acting upon them deprives them of their free agency. But *White Noise* is no classic naturalist novel; it is a subversion of the genre played out through the mask thereof. The emerging scenic action of *White Noise* crystallizes all the tiny intimations of disaster that crowd Jack's consciousness, and that come fully into view in the novel's second section, "The Airborne Toxic Event" – the evasive name not of a natural but of a human effect whose peculiarity is that it is the unintended consequence of the desire of the technologically sophisticated to insulate themselves from the enduring cockroach. "The Airborne Toxic Event" is DeLillo's dark comic rebuke of first world hubris, an expression of a controlling structural irony that definitively subverts the conventional critical distinction of character and setting. Setting, in this book, is character become a runaway cancer, intention out of control.

Cutting against the grain of this ecological theme of man as self-victimizer is a countertheme initiated by the romantic poets, elaborated and fully embraced in the high modernist ethos of Yeats, Joyce, Pound, and Stevens: the theme of freedom and dignity aesthetically won, the artist as hero. In the philosophical tradition out of Kant's *Critique of Judgment,* running through the cultural theories of neo-Kantian idealists from Schiller to Marcuse, culminating in literary theory in Northrop Frye's *Anatomy of Criticism:* the theme of aesthetic humanism, modernist culture's last ditch defense of man against the technologies of modernization. In art, so goes the plea, lies the salvation of our humanity – character shielded from setting, free agency and the autonomy of intention restored.

White Noise is a meditative sort of narrative conducted by a cultural anatomist in the wake of Keats, capitalism, and the revolutions in electronics. When Jack thinks, sees, and feels in the categories of art – the book is liberally peppered with such moments – Jack the victim is magically transmuted into Jack the victor, the poised angel of observation whose values are superior to those of the mass culture he anatomizes. The more impressive effects of Jack's aesthetic consciousness come through with a minimum of rhetorical fanfare: They are effects of the counternarrative sort, spatial rather than temporal, produced with quiet painterly eloquence and the haunting precision of black-and-white photography. These are the signature moments of Jack as artist, working in the mode of Antonioni, whose camera eye (with sharp point in *Red Desert*) repeatedly creates painterly and photographic effects, infinitesimally frozen frames, an antinarrative cinema dedicated like Jack's antinarrative narrative to the disquieting image removed from the stream of time, a thing of beauty forever whose power to mesmerize is owed to its menacing context, the story that moves silently underground.

These small moments of the aesthetic image in *White Noise* tend to be put into the background (where they belong and do their insidious work) by big interpretive moments when Jack sees his world demanding to be read, as if his salvation (a recollection of Christian allegory) depended upon it. In this register, Jack's high cultural perspective would redeem him from the cultural ecosystems of the mass media that threaten to rule his consciousness, and would provide a consolation of spirit – the Dylar effect of high culture – even as he faces fatal exposure to the terrible black cloud. Nowhere is Jack's aesthetic power more flashily in evidence than when he lifts the trash bag from the trash compactor: "An oozing cube of semi-mangled cans, clothes hangers, animal-bones and other refuse . . . a horrible clotted mass of hair, soap, ear swabs, crushed roaches, flip-top rings, sterile pads smeared with pus and bacon fat, strands of frayed dental floss, fragments of ballpoint pen refills, tooth picks still displaying bits of impaled food." He wonders if he has finally encountered the "dark underside of consumer consciousness." He says, in his revulsion, "the full stench hit me with shocking force," but the stench is not quite full because the stinking chaos is mediated, shaped into the speech of a sharp-tongued familiar. The oozing cube of garbage sits there "like an ironic modern sculpture, massive, squat, mocking."

Constantly shadowing Jack's arty self-consciousness is an unconscious epistemology of consumption. Jack tends to "see" commodities, and with their right names attached. He notes a "camouflage jacket with Velcro closures"; "a family of five [getting] out of a Datsun Maxima"; he tells us that his "newspaper is delivered by a middle-aged Iranian driving a Nissan Sentra"; somebody is wearing a "Gore-Tex jacket"; he feels a "chill pass through the Hong Kong polyester" of his pajamas. In each of these instances – funny to us but not to Jack – Jack is the object of DeLillo's wit, the postmodern anatomist postmodernized, and so become the automaton of consumer society: Sometimes the object of Jack's wit, in these instances brand names creep into the syntax of his perceptions. The brand name: the lens of his vision, the source of his power to name and in naming create the world of typical experience. The brand name: a curious human bond, the stuff of community. And not even the cute malapropisms of his kids can escape. One of them says, "It's called the sun's corolla." Another responds, "I thought corolla was a car." The precocious Heinrich rejoins, "Everything is a car." In desperate conversation with Murray – he knows that he's been decisively exposed to the toxic cloud – Jack says, "I want to live," and Murray replies with a brief filmographic description: "From the Robert Wise film of the same name, with Susan Hayward as Barbara Graham, a convicted murderess. Aggressive jazz score by Johnny Mandel." Heinrich was wrong; everything's a movie.

Against such odds Jack's aesthetic sensibility plays to win. Gazing upon his "ironic modern sculpture" he resembles an earlier gazer upon the ironies of spatial art. "What habits, fetishes, addictions, inclinations? What solitary acts? behavioral ruts?" The exact rhythmic echo of Keats's excited questions in the poem about the Grecian urn is parodic, all right, but with a difference. Jack's parody establishes a decidedly deflating commentary on Keats's enthusiasm with its unflattering reduction of the urn to garbage ("Thou shalt remain . . . a friend to man"), and its delightfully grotesque translation of Keats's idealized "more happy, happy love" to "I found crayon drawings of a figure with full breasts and male genitals," "I found a banana skin with a tampon inside" – as if to say, look what I, impoverished postmodern poet, have to deal with. At the same time a subtle compact with Keats is made in the covert celebration of the power (Jack's and John's both) of aesthetic redemption, transcendence to the plane of art. Garbage mediated by literary history becomes a kind of literary text. The isolation of the postmodern moment is alleviated as the individual talent makes contact with tradition. That "ironic modern sculpture" of compacted garbage is a figure for *White Noise* itself, whose mocking irony consists in its refusal to let its readers off the hook of self-reliance by giving them an omniscient perspective: never telling them, however subtly, how to live, what to think.

The difficulty of levitating garbage to the plane of art is nothing compared to the problem posed by the toxic cloud. The second section of the novel offers us two narratives: the gripping plot of mass threat, mass evacuation, and mass escape, shadowed by an overplot of sensibility, a narrative whose end is also escape – to make looming death hospitable by making it beautiful. What Jack glimpses in his first look through the binoculars lies at the distant edge of his categories: "a heavy black mass hanging in the air beyond the river, more or less shapeless." Heinrich tells his father that the radio calls it a "feathery plume," but Heinrich, like his father, comments on its strangeness: "Like a shapeless growing thing" – is this the beginning of a sci-fi movie? – "A dark black breathing thing of smoke." Others in the family inhale the media mediation: "Can you see the feathery plume?" one of the other kids says. What are they "doing about the actual plume," wonders another. The media revises the image: from "feathery plume" to "black billowing cloud" and then, in a forsaking of all concreteness, in a leap to the plane of abstraction, "the airborne toxic event." A character in *Ratner's Star* remarks that we "can measure the gravity of events by tracing the increasingly abstract nature of the terminology." The perfected abstract euphemism, the state's poetry of concealment, offers no consolation; for those who can read it, it tells the awful truth in the very act of cover-up.

The interior narrative of Jack's aesthetic sensibility, never shared in dialogue, represents another kind of journey to abstraction and containment, whose end is neither truth nor lie but conversion of the real for the ends of private consolation. The scene of the toxic spill at the railroad switching yard becomes "operatic chaos"; the thick mist arching over the scene recalls "some grand confection of patriotic music." In the midst of *evacuation*, Jack sees *exodus* – people on foot, sadly burdened with various belongings, crossing a highway overpass. Jack thinks "epic quality" – and suddenly these people become for him "part of some ancient destiny, connected in doom and ruin to a whole history of people walking across wasted landscapes." On the highway he sees the aftermath of a terrible wreck, bloody people, collapsed metal, blood-soaked snow – "all washed in a strong and eerie light," the whole taking on the "eloquence of a formal composition." Passing a hastily evacuated gas station, pumps unlocked, Jack finds himself in a museum, thinking "the tools and pottery of some pueblo civilization, bread in the oven, table set for three, a mystery to haunt the generations." Finally, the thing itself, no longer "shapeless," no longer a "thing" but a literary memory, "like some death ship in a Norse legend," a spectacle assuming its honored place in the "grandness of a sweeping event" – and Jack is reminded by it of the "operatic" scene at the switching yard; reminded of the "people trudging across the snowy overpass," "a tragic army of the dispossessed," reminded, in other words, of the recent aestheticizing history of his own mind.

The narrator tries hard to disillusion himself. "This was a death made in the laboratory . . . this was not history we were witnessing." But it *is* history, of a monstrous kind, beyond our traditional categories of familiarization. Under the duress of the event Jack has told us of his need to experience sublimity whatever the source; to make grand, sweeping, literary sense of the good old-fashioned sort, when there were heroes; to become part of a tradition extending from unnamed Norse poets, to Keats, to himself, deployer of literary and art history, poet's critic. In his most imaginative moment, he leaps into the future to assume the role of archaeologist digging into the ruins his civilization will leave; the imagined dig becoming romantic adventure, conferring mystery while repressing the harsher question: Who or what is responsible for the dispossession of the dispossessed?

Not once does DeLillo permit his narrator reflection upon his own proclivity for ennobling conversion. The implication is that the aestheticizing habit is Jack's personally cultivated state of self-consciousness, which would function as a saving balance to his banal, semi-stupid brand name apprehension of the world. DeLillo's critique of high-cultural Jack is implicit. When the camp of evacuees is threatened by a shift in wind currents, a stampede erupts, which Jack is quick to invest with grandiosity – "like the fall of a colonial capital to dedicated rebels. A great surging drama with elements of humiliation and guilt." Precisely at that moment, his second up-close sight of the toxic cloud, the heroic veneer of his perception is stripped away and Jack's high art becomes a stunning reminder of what it most desires to oppose: media jargon. Jack's aesthetic way is another kind of euphemistic escape, literary feedback doing the work of a mind ill at ease in its setting, straining to get out, and telling us in the process, without meaning to, how beside the point its high cultural values are: telling us, without meaning to, that literary feedback – the cultivated media experience of the highly cultivated – is not much different from mass media feedback, with the difference lying all in the favor of the mass media.

In the hybrid character of Jack Gladney, DeLillo plays a condensed variation on the method of *Ulysses,* with Joyce's high-order phenomenological seismograph, the sensitive Bloom, become Jack, a richly registered impression of postmodern culture, the vehicle of the novel's "naturalistic" surface; and Dedalus also become Jack, the high literary leavening and clarification of chaotic contemporaneity, however sterile. The Jack-as-Bloom socialized in the ambience of the postmodern arts of advertising rebukes the Jack of high art, the Jack-as-Dedalus, with something more believable, more "natural" – another kind of mediation which makes allusions to Norse legend seem absurd. The revenge of mass culture: The cloud "resembled a national promotion for death, a multi-million dollar campaign backed by radio spots, heavy print and billboard, TV saturation."

"We faced each other, propped on elbows, like a sculpture of lounging philosophers in a classical academy." Thus Jack, as he and Babette lie in bed, she about to reveal the sordid little tale of Dylar, he thinking about a trip to ancient Greece via the high Italian Renaissance, remembering perhaps Raphael's *School of Athens*. And after he's been told by a medical technician that tests show traces in his bloodstream of the spilled by-product of the airborne toxic event, and that he should carry his computer-coded results to his doctor (because "Your doctor knows the symbols"), Jack walks out of the clinic directly into the pathos of a nineteenth-century novel: "How literary, I thought peevishly. Streets thick with the details of impulsive life as the hero ponders the latest phase in his dying." This latter, literary reminiscence, then succeeded immediately by unreflective media-speak, in the rhetoric of the weather report: quotation unawares, pastiche undeliberate, no parody intended, no critical distance won. "It was a partially cloudy day with winds diminishing toward sunset."

Precisely at that moment (in Chapter 36) with weatherman jargon welling up through his voice, this human collage of styles – this loquacious product of, and advertisement for, the American cultural ecosystem – appears to free himself by turning deliberate storyteller, by seizing his culture's most powerful medium of the image, the TV commercial, as the stuff of literary narrative and the occasion of intervention. Jack is here postmodernism's own parodic Homer, no longer media subject but media subjugator, telling us the tale of the electronic tribe. The extended family that phones together stays together – a Trimline, a white Princess; a people, a nation:

> That night I walked the streets of Blacksmith. The glow of blue-eyed TVs. The voices on the touch-tone phones. Far away the grandparents huddle in a chair, eagerly sharing the receiver as carrier waves modulate into audible signals. It is the voice of their grand-

son, the growing boy whose face appears in the snapshots set
around the phone. Joy rushes to their eyes but it is misted over,
infused with a sad and complex knowing. What is the youngster
saying to them? His wretched complexion makes him unhappy? He
wants to leave school and work full-time at Foodland, bagging
groceries? He tells them he *likes* to bag groceries. It is the one thing
in life he finds satisfying. . . . I like it gramma, it's totally un-
threatening, it's how I want to spend my life. And so they listen
sadly, loving him all the more, their faces pressed against the sleek
Trimline, the white Princess in the bedroom, the plain brown Rotary
in granddad's paneled basement hideaway.

"What happens after the commercial ends?" Jack had asked
himself earlier, at the beginning of the chapter, when he'd aborted
his blow-by-blow replay of that same AT&T ad, "Reach out and
touch someone!" And now we know the answer. At the end of the
chapter Jack reimagines the commercial in a caustically comic
excursion through TV land, which ends with a personal meditation that evokes a traditional ominous symbolism, a key vein of
romantic imagery, passing from Poe's story of A. Gordon Pym,
trapped hopelessly in the Antarctic, through Joyce's December
snows in "The Dead," to Thomas Mann's *Magic Mountain*. Jack's
postmodern music begins with a quotation of the classic weather
report and concludes with a complex allusion to classic literature's
allegorical winters: "Clouds race across the westering moon, the
seasons change in somber montage, going deeper into winter still-
ness, a landscape of silence and ice."

Then one thing more, a single-sentence paragraph which ends
Chapter 36: "Your doctor knows the symbols" – a repetition of
what Jack had been told by the medical technician who knows the
bad news, and who was given to us as a foreshadowing double
only a few pages earlier: "He was a mild-eyed fellow with a poor
complexion and reminded me of the boys at the supermarket who
stand at the end of the checkout counter bagging merchandise."
The medical technician, a minor character in Jack's novel (so goes
the fiction of the first-person mode) unexpectedly haunts a fiction
within a fiction. Jack's masterful send-up story of the TV commercial is undermined by the protean messenger of death who gets
inside the safe place of his imagination – assuming the shape of

the acne-struck bag boy, messenger of the last word that undoes all words, including those of Jack's parody.

Jack's failure to dominate the art of the TV ad – not his beloved euphemisms of high art – brings him, curiously, closest to himself as a voice whose integrity is sustained against the erosions of all mediation – whether high literary or high Madison Avenue – a brooding presence whose abiding source is death-obsession. The authentic Jack is the vulnerable self who flees himself through the cover-ups of his acute learnedness, his satire, parody, and general all-around wittiness; he is the man who fears for his wife and children – and whose attachment to them is not ironic; whose devotion – the book's deepest mystery, its most shocking dimension – is actually supported by the supermarket ("where we wait together, regardless of age, our carts stocked with brightly colored goods"), by the shopping mall, where his kids become guides to his "endless well-being" – "I was one of them, shopping, at last" – and by the arts of advertising which give him entry into religious solace, even "aura." "Aura": the salient quality that Murray ascribed to our experience of "the most photographed barn"; the emanation of a source, the nimbus of the real, the indicator of depth, origin, and authenticity – everything, in other words, presumably unavailable to the postmodern world of reproduction, simulation, repetition, and image – suddenly and stunningly restored by the supermarket, the mall, the poetry of media glut.

That night at the camp for evacuees of Blacksmith, Jack hears one of the kids mumble something in her sleep; he leans over to catch the meaning, convinced it will be a revelation of innocence and his route to some unshakable comfort. She speaks again – this time clearly, as if in ecstatic chant, a ritualized utterance that he receives not in corrosive satiric perspective – which would have been the conventional literary payoff in this moment – but with amazement and awe:

Toyota Celica.
The utterance was beautiful and mysterious, gold-shot with looming wonder. It was like the name of an ancient power in the sky, tablet-carved in cuneiform. It made me feel that something hovered. But how could this be? A simple brand name, an ordinary

111

car. How could these near-nonsense words, murmured in a child's restless sleep, make me sense a meaning, a presence? . . . Whatever its source, the utterance struck me with the impact of a moment of splendid transcendence.

Each of these moments – at the supermarket, at the mall, hearing Steffie talk in her sleep – is delivered with mordantly styled humor because it's almost impossible for Jack to speak any other way: He's doomed with critical knowledge of his life's deep support systems. Nevertheless, there is always something else in the voice, not easy to define because in books of this sort we don't expect domestic commitment or a sense of wonder on behalf of the culture's binding power. At such moments in *White Noise*, DeLillo's readers – sophisticates, like him, of corrosive truth – are given an alternative. Would we prefer that Jack give up the supermarket, the mall, his family, the nights gathered around the TV, for another, chilling guarantor of community, who lurks in the background of *White Noise*, as in the background of a number of modernist literary monuments – the specter of the totalitarian, the gigantic charismatic figure who triggers our desire to give in, to merge our frightened selves in his frightening authority? Hitler, another kind of epic hero, voice of national solidarity, is the other object of Jack's awe.

At the novel's end Jack meets Willy Mink, Babette's betrayer, the corrupt agent of Dylar. The plot that Jack hatches in order to kill Willy Mink embodies his dream of existential self-determination, precisely what his culture denies him. But he who would be master of plot, at the end, becomes, again, plot's creature, as he plays, again, the role of the clown of plot.

Willy Mink is what the precariously centered Jack might become, postmodern man's essence, and our culture's re-formation of the meaning of madness. Willy Mink is a voice without a center, a jumbled bunch of fragments from various contemporary jargons, mostly emanating from the TV he sits in front of with the sound turned down, overdosing on Dylar – the pure American product who speaks these sentences:

Some of these sure-footed bighorns have been equipped with
radio transmitters. . . . The heat from your hand will actually make
the gold-leafing stick to the wax-paper.
This is what the scientists don't understand, scrubbing their
smocks with Woolite. Not that I have anything personal against
death from our vantage point high atop Metropolitan County Sta-
dium.

Willy Mink is the promised end of a journey that began on the
Mayflower, the shocking *telos* of the third-person ideal, the "I"
converted to bits and pieces of language not his own. Sitting in
front of the TV, throwing fistfuls of Dylar at his mouth, babbling,
Willy Mink is a compacted image of consumerism in the society of
the electronic media, a figure of madness, but our figure of madness. Is Willy Mink a just image of postmodern community in
America, a sick representation thereof, or both?

America's profoundest philosopher of community, Josiah Royce,
believed that true community consisted in collective consciousness
of historical process; community as memory of a significant extended past which all members hold in common and as hope for
the future – an expectation that the historical process will con-
tinue to be a story that possesses sense and coherence, and that the
future will, like the past, be a nurturing time for cohesive values
and actions. In Royce's rigorous terms, it is difficult to speak of
postmodern "community," unless we are willing to take absolutely
seriously the proposition that postmodernism came over on the
Mayflower. If we cannot, then we are left with this rejoinder to
Royce: Communities have to start somewhere, a community's collective memory needs to have beginnings to recollect. The era of
the shopping mall, the supermarket, the fast-food restaurants, and
the ritual family gatherings around the TV is in its infancy. But
who knows? One day we might say that at the close of the twentieth century we began to discover the binding power, the comforts
of our new Roman Church. Hard to say, before it comes to pass, in
all its laws, liturgies, and forms of behavior, that it will do any
more damage than the old.

Notes on Contributors

Paul Cantor is Professor of English at the University of Virginia. He is the author of *Shakespeare's Rome, Creature and Creator,* and *Shakespeare: Hamlet.*

Thomas J. Ferraro is an Assistant Professor of English at Duke University. He has published essays on ethnicity, gender, and capitalism in twentieth-century literature and film. He is finishing a book tentatively entitled *Blood in the Marketplace: Ethnic Narrative and Modern America.*

Frank Lentricchia, Katherine Everett Gilbert Professor of English at Duke University and editor of the *South Atlantic Quarterly,* is the author of *The Gaiety of Language* (1968), *Robert Frost: Modern Poetics and the Landscapes of Self* (1975), *After the New Criticism* (1980), *Criticism and Social Change* (1983), and *Ariel and the Police* (1988). He is the editor of *Robert Frost: A Bibliography, 1913–1974* (1976, with Melissa Lentricchia), *Critical Terms for Literary Study* (1990, with Thomas McLaughlin) and *Introducing Don DeLillo* (1991).

Michael Valdez Moses is Assistant Professor of English at Duke University. He has published articles on contemporary third world and postcolonial literature and on nineteenth- and twentieth-century British fiction. He is completing a book tentatively entitled *Tragedy and Modernity: The Novel and the End of History.*

Bibliographical Note

White Noise was published by Viking in 1985; a portion of the novel appeared in *Vanity Fair*. In 1986, Viking printed the paperback edition (Penguin Books) with identical pagination.

The novel was widely reviewed:

Antioch Review (Fall 1985)
Atlantic Monthly (Feb. 1985)
Commonweal (April 5, 1985)
Fantasy Review (Aug. 1985)
Hudson Review (Summer 1985)
Los Angeles Times (Jan. 13, 1985)
Library Journal (Feb. 1, 1985)
Maclean's Magazine (April 1, 1985)
The Nation (Feb. 2, 1985)
The New Republic (Feb. 1985)
New Statesman (Jan. 17, 1986)
Newsweek (Jan. 21, 1985)
New York Review of Books (March 14, 1985)
New York Times (Jan. 7, 1985)
New York Times Book Review (Jan. 13, 1985)
Observer (London) (Feb. 9, 1986)
Partisan Review (Summer 1986)
Quill and Quire (April 1985)
Saturday Review (March-April 1985)
The Spectator (Feb. 22, 1986)
Time (Jan. 31, 1985)
USA Today (Jan. 11, 1985)
Village Voice (April 30, 1985)
Washington Post Book World (Jan. 13, 1985)
Wilson Library Quarterly (May 1985)

For essay-length treatment of the novel, see the appropriate chapter in Tom LeClair's *In the Loop: Don DeLillo and the Systems Novel* (Urbana: University of Illinois Press, 1987), and John Frow's essay in my collection *Introducing Don DeLillo* (Durham, N.C.: Duke University Press, 1991). Frow's piece appeared originally in the *South Atlantic Quarterly*'s special number on DeLillo (Spring 1990).